Snow Petrel

JON TUCKER

STORM BAY BOOKS

ALSO BY JON TUCKER

Those Snake Island Kids
Those Eco-Pirate Kids
Those Shipwreck Kids
Those Sugar-Barge Kids

Text © 2011 Jon Tucker

Photographs © 2011 Matt Tucker, Ben Tucker, Debra Shapiro and
      Barbara Tucker

ISBN   9781723769429

First Published by
Forty Degrees South, Tasmania

This edition by Storm Bay Books 2018

FRONT COVER IMAGE
Snow Petrel in Antarctic waters

BACK COVER IMAGES
Snow Petrel in the Furious Fifties
Snow Petrel in a Cape Denison blizzard

How often is a father allowed to crew for his sons on an ocean passage to one of the most remote parts of the world? Especially when that destination is statistically the windiest place on the planet, and the vessel is a small home-built, unsponsored yacht without much of the equipment to be expected for a voyage across the most feared ocean in the world.

This is more than a simple travel voyage. It paints a picture of the human side of sailing – of the camaraderie and the misery. Enmeshed in a tale full of surprises is a host of historical and technical detail, as well as the parallel story of a family of five boys home-schooled aboard a traditional ocean going yacht.

In the twelve years since this voyage occurred, no sailing vessel of *any* size has repeated the feat. The following pages prove what can be achieved with a paucity of money and a wealth of human spirit.

New Zealand Maid

JON TUCKER is a Kiwi ex-teacher turned adventurer whose home-built traditional ketch *New Zealand Maid* is the only home he and his wife Barbara owned for over thirty years. In addition to building a stunning vessel, they have raised a family of five high-achieving sons and have extensively sailed the waters of New Zealand, Australia and the Pacific.

ACKNOWLEDGEMENTS

There are two journeys associated with the creation of this book. Neither would have succeeded without the generosity and support of a significant network of friends and even virtual strangers.

The voyage itself was hugely aided by the gifts, advice and loans of many well-wishers. Some, like Mike Harris, Don and Margie MacIntyre – and of course my incredibly capable wife Barbara – feature significantly in the narrative. But many others deserve our thanks for their contribution to the adventure. Chris Short and Shane Procter cheerfully tolerated our disruptions to the South Haven Marina and Mermaid Café during our hectic preparations. Nick Gales, Kieran Lawton and Erryn Reeder provided enough Antarctic clothing to make up for our significant shortfall. Rod Paine, the MacIntyres, Donough Benson, Tony Forman, Tim Walters and Russell Streckfuss helped out with extra equipment for the boat. Ian Balmer loaded us up with enough emergency rations to take the pressure off our weather-enforced delays. Amanda Beecroft and Andrew Climie gave invaluable assistance with our medical preparations. Steve Reid, Scott Lachlan and Gilbert Cesa provided weather and ice reports to supplement the information Mike Harris and Barbara were supplying. And all the team at the French base deserve special thanks. Particularly Ariane Richesse and Patrice Godon for substituting a red carpet in place of red tape. Ultimately of course, the voyage was Ben's. I hold him in awe.

As for the second journey, the writing and publishing of a book is not without its hurdles. In particular my editor Janet Upcher's enthusiasm (coupled with Chris Gallagher's very positive response at the Tasmanian Writers' Centre) helped counter the publishing industry's hesitant response to my experimental presentation devices. Thanks also must go to the hidden editors – the very capable and experienced maritime friends who picked their way through the manuscript in search of the little oversights which are so easy to miss. Rolf Bjelke and Debra Shapiro off *Northern Light*, Jocelyn Foganolo and Neil Lamont, Alain Pottier, Philippe Dordhain, Court Hobday, Fred and Jocelyn Westrupp and – naturally - Ben, Barbara and Matt Tucker all managed to pick up small but significant typos and factual omissions in the script. I owe huge credit to Matt for most of the photographs. He has a true artist's eye, and was a wonderful crewmate as well. Barbara Tucker and Debra Shapiro also supplied photographs I have included in the book. And in the end, at Forty Degrees South Publishing, Warren Boyles and especially Kent Whitmore have my hearty thanks for taking the stress out of the last leg of the whole adventure.

To Babs

for understanding me better than myself

And to Ben

for saying yes

INTRODUCTION

Snow Petrel consists of two quite separate books. One is an extraordinary tale of sailing – well outside the genre of most of the sailing books many of us have read. The second provides a wonderful insight into a very special family.

High latitude sailing is the province of a very small and select group. They are typically stern of face, eccentric and larger than life. Their voyages are legendary – crowds of adoring fans herald their departure and return.

In contrast, there was the voyage of *Snow Petrel*. There was no fanfare, no sponsorship, no square-jawed gazes into distant horizons. No – in the book you will learn that his voyage was the fulfilment of an unassuming, understated and extraordinarily capable young man; Ben Tucker.

The second side of this book is the story of the extraordinary Tucker family; five boys – all wonderful characters in their own right – raised on the lovely ketch *New Zealand Maid* by their inseparable parents – Jon and Barbara. Together they share a love of a simple unencumbered life on the sea that revolves around people and places – not possessions and wealth!

In this book, through the adventure launched by his eldest son, Jon provides a reflection of what really counts in families and relationships. It's rare to share in a trip like this without having to read through ego and shared recollections.

To me this is what makes this book really special. And rare !!

Dr Nick Gales - *Director, Australian Antarctic Division*

CONTENTS

PHASE 1

Chaos and Departure

Everyone knows it's almost impossible to keep plans secret. Especially plans as extreme as Ben's.

He had his reasons for staying tight-lipped. Better to stay quiet from the start than shout to the world and suffer the finger-pointing of failure. His philosophy had merits.

But human nature is predictable. It took only a few confidential leaks for the rumours to start. Ben had hinted his plans to a few close friends and before long the visitors began hanging around the marina. Pretending to know nothing, they were cautious in their questioning. And it wasn't hard to find something to ask about. The first clue was that Ben had re-named his little home-built steel sloop Snow Petrel. *Then there were the modifications. Hull-strengthening, rig-strengthening and the perspex domes. Not just one dome but two – the sort that are used for visibility in the ice. And of course there was all the polystyrene insulation.*

Ben's standard response was a vague reference to 'cruising south for a few weeks'. In most circumstances this would raise little comment. If for example Snow Petrel *was back in our former home port – Wellington – there would have been plenty of options with half of New Zealand to the south, and then further islands. But we were not in Wellington any longer. Our little marina at Kettering in Tasmania was one of the southernmost locations in Australia. A cruise south was going to take Ben about five hours before he ran out of land. And from then on there would be no islands, just the most feared waters in the world for nearly three thousand kilometres.*

4 JANUARY 2006
0955 HRS

Customs is booked to clear us at 1000 hrs. Two pleasant young uniformed women step aboard right on time, confiding that they enjoy the chance to drive down the Channel to Kettering. Apparently it's a diversion from more mundane Hobart office-work and cruise-liners. They're quite relaxed as we fill in our paperwork in the cockpit, after clearing a space among the still chaotic jumble of provisions. We even joke about the need to fill in forms for a journey that is unlikely to land us in a foreign port. However remembering a parallel occasion more than a decade ago – sailing continuously for three weeks through international waters and returning to the same port amid a howl of indignation from customs authorities – we agree that it's best to do everything by the book. Who knows, after all, where we may eventually wash up?

'It's times like these I love my job!' says the blonde one as they gather their papers and slip off up to the Mermaid Café from where they can idly observe our continuing preparations over a cappuccino.

Barbara and I have five sons. In hindsight it seems rather ill-advised, especially as the only home we have ever owned is the traditional ketch we built when we were young. But if we were to have our time again we would do it pretty much the same.

One thing about raising a family of this size with so much time together is that everyone has to pull their weight. Even at ten years of age, Matt – the youngest – was expected to stand helming watches in the Southern Ocean on our protest voyage to Moruroa. And we had to trust him. Not surprisingly, all the boys have grown into adulthood maintaining close seagoing interests.

Ben's love of the sea began at a young age, and almost bordered on obsession. Anything maritime was fair game to him. Small wonder that he left home at seventeen to study navigation in England. With a foreign-going mate's ticket on big P&O ships, his career looked set. But no, sail was his passion and soon found him working as chief officer on the square rigged Soren Larsen *and later single-handing his engineless twenty-six foot* Reiger *from New Zealand to Australia where he ended up teaching navigation at the Australian Maritime College.*

1030 HRS

With the formalities over, we undergo a mental shift. Although there is still a lot of gear to stow, we feel as if the voyage has begun. Little *Snow Petrel* is staggering under her payload and the white waterline is now under-water,

Our preparations proceed in second gear, South Haven Marina, Tasmania

leaving only the freshly painted red topsides for the slight westerly chop to splash against. After so many weeks of working against the clock, we now agree to abandon the idea of fully stowing before departure. After all, Ben reasons, we have several hours of sheltered waterways to continue the last-minute stuff, and there is always the option of anchoring before launching ourselves into the Southern Ocean.

A small crowd is gathering. Ben has expressly avoided making an event of this departure and is relieved that the onlookers are mostly fellow live-aboards and a few close friends. The mood is pleasantly merry, and there is plenty of laughter. Chris, a mate who happens to own this marina, rushes off after eyeing our tiny New Zealand flag and the correspondingly oversized Australian one. A few moments later he returns with an enormous Tasmanian flag – a magnificent Blue Ensign defaced with a red lion crest.

I must admit to having known very little about Antarctica. At least not until October 2005. Boats sail to the Peninsula, but I had been more interested in sailing our own boat to Alaska after son number three, Josh, sailed there on a super-yacht and brought home some amazing images. Barbara outspokenly favoured the tropics, even though I pointed out that there are plenty of tropical waters between here and Alaska.

A Frenchman once confided that the easiest way to get to Antarctica was via South America. He had crossed Drake's Passage to the Peninsula twice, waiting for a weather window and doing the hop with only two nights at sea.

As a family member I was one of the chosen few to be officially aware that Ben was keen on a trip to the ice. Somewhere. It seemed logical to assume that he would probably be doing the mid-latitude 'run to South America and turn right' option. A very substantial cruise, but one that potentially could avoid those dreaded giant seas of the deep Southern Ocean. Especially if the Frenchman's advice was for real.

So on that late October morning, on a mountainside high above Hobart, Ben dropped it to me that his favoured destination for the summer was to be Cape Denison. Being a Kiwi, the name meant little to me. In my school days Scott and Amundsen were the recognised Antarctic heroes, while Mawson – the Australian hero – didn't rate a mention. From my meagre knowledge base, mainland Antarctica to the south of Australia and New Zealand was essentially a coast of ice-cliffs hidden behind a field of impenetrable pack ice.

1050 HRS

I'm amazed how calm and happy Barbara appears. She laughs and jokes with the rest of them as I hand her a plastic bag of smelly socks and undies that Ben and Matt have decided to jettison rather than wash at sea. To an onlooker she would seem to be waving us off for an afternoon fishing trip, not farewelling her husband and two sons on a voyage from which they may never return.

We have our wet weather bib-front over-trousers on now and have hurriedly gathered any loose objects from the cockpit for temporary stowage. Amanda's little red sloop is already hovering beyond the break-water to accompany us for a few miles down the channel. It's time to make a move.

Everything seems to happen so quickly. There are no tears, only a hasty hug for Barbara from the three of us. One or two cameras are filming as we gather the lines and reverse out, sharing another joke and a lot of waving. Ben is determined to be under full sail as swiftly as possible. He has always hated engines, even as a small child.

The past six weeks had been a blur of chaotic activity. I've been through quite a few voyage preparations before, often to an impossible deadline and usually ending in a departure which was not quite as well prepared as I would have liked. Barbara and I became hooked on lists. There would be an A-list

Shortly before departure, all self-conscious about our haircuts. From left—me, Ben and Matt

and a B-list. The first was the 'must-do's and the second was the 'hope-to's. We also used to rate our preparations on a four gear basis. We'd start at a leisurely rate – first gear – with a glass of wine at the end of a moderate day's achievements and no alarm clock. By third gear we'd be into ten hour days with a little night-time spotlit action. Usually at around the week-to-go phase with about half the A-list complete we'd hit top gear and with two days left it would be overdrive or panic mode. From then to departure we would seldom have had more than two or three hours' sleep.

This lot of preparations was rather different. It was Ben's trip and we were initially just his reinforcements. Ben hates paperwork so there were no lists. We progressively began to feel that we were operating in a vacuum. Three weeks before Christmas Barbara, Matt and I had begun suffering from list withdrawal symptoms. There seemed to be no end to the work. His proposed departure date of 20 December seemed no closer, and some sort of priority ranking would have to happen. At last he printed us a single list – forty jobs to go, some quite major.

And so a B-list was also born of necessity. A revised departure deadline of New Year's Day was set. Beyond that date there would be little point departing this season.

1130 HRS

Matt and I have sailed only once on *Snow Petrel* before this departure. That was ten days earlier on Christmas day in a gale. We are used to the lofty gaff rig of our ketch, *New Zealand Maid*. In contrast, *Snow Petrel* seems as responsive and light as a big dinghy. To be tiller steering again after years of wheel steering is a novelty. But Ben has his Fleming self steering quickly hooked up. Like all good skippers Ben loves his servo-pendulum like a favourite crew-member, and has named him 'Sooty'. We quickly learn to love him too. He eats nothing and craves little more than some occasional attention and a gentle tweak from time to time.

As we harden sheets for a tight-reach down D'Entrecasteaux Channel, Amanda and Craig shadow us aboard *Aerandir* for the first half hour. We manage to get Matt's video camera across to them with a bit of fancy manoeuvring and they capture some good footage before peeling off into Peppermint Bay for lunch. We sail on alone though I see Barbara in our car, hopscotching her way down the coastal road, parking briefly to watch us pass each accessible beach. She phones to say she'll be on the end of the Gordon jetty, so we roll away the genoa and sail slowly past for a final goodbye. It must be hard for her but she seems cheerful. We've almost always voyaged together and it's a new experience for her to be the stay-at-home wife and mother.

'You should have your harnesses on by now,' she calls. She's right, though we're still in sheltered waters, and we take her advice as we wave our final goodbyes. The sou'wester is building to 25 knots, and *Snow Petrel* becomes lively as the Channel widens.

It wasn't in Ben's original plans to have us with him. He had intended to take only his brother Dan as crew. There's only a year between our two eldest boys and they have voyaged together enough to trust each other absolutely. But Dan and another brother, Sam, were committed to a launching deadline for their jointly owned trimaran.

For a trip like this Ben had to believe in his crew. Josh, the next brother, was also tied up with a serious sailing commitment – delivering a race yacht around Cape Horn. So we suggested that he should consider taking Matt, the baby of our five. Matt had always been one of those rare individuals who from a young age would stand his watch without complaint no matter how miserable or horrific the conditions, then calmly settle in his bunk with a book and walkman. He may have been a little casual about life at times, but for a trip like this he'd be gold.

Our last view of Barbara on the Gordon jetty ... and of the sight of green for a while too

With ten years between them, Ben had never really got to know his kid brother well. He had sailed off to England at seventeen when Matt was only seven. They had voyaged together on occasions but hadn't built the relationship that Ben had with Dan. But what were the alternatives? It wasn't that he lacked friends. There were many good friends who would possibly have risked this voyage with him. But for a trip this extreme, with so much at stake and at such short notice, he was reluctant to offer anyone else a position. Especially as it would involve total commitment towards preparations, during the weeks before Christmas. So Matt it was to be, and he flew in willingly from Auckland like a lamb to the slaughter.

Barbara and I threw ourselves behind the project too, as parents do. But it took its toll on our relationship as we worked long hours to the detriment of our own needs. It was Barbara who understood even better than me how deeply I craved a fuller part in the venture. She knew full well that it would be a safer journey with three on board. And so I crawled to Ben with a proposition at midnight three weeks before Christmas. If I were to offer myself as cabin-boy, promising to fully recognise Ben's ownership of the voyage, would he consider including me? It took him five days of procrastination and several soul-searching conversations with his mother before I knew his verdict.

And so it was that Barbara was to wave off half her immediate family on a crazy voyage into the unknown.

1630 HRS

We're taking turns to stow the provisions and gear as we sail. Lunch has been a haphazard affair, and there is so much re-stowing to do. In a small boat pitching into a head-sea at a 25 degree heel, this is not easy. Ahead lies Dover, then Southport and finally Recherche Bay. We discuss it and Ben makes the decision. We will anchor in the Southport deep hole and get everything ship-shape before continuing into open waters.

There is a grey area about movements after clearing customs. We have never received an unequivocal direction from any authority regarding stopping between clearance and departing territorial waters. The vague impression we have been given is that there is about twenty-four hours' grace, as long as no further physical contact with people is made. Beyond that time, the authorities like to be informed.

At 1800 hrs we drop the pick and begin a systematic re-stow. It takes till midnight but it's worth the effort. From chaos comes orderliness. Gear forward is lashed down on the double bunk which now serves as a giant shelf. Provisions are stored in order of expected consumption, and their locations recorded. Items of safety equipment are given accessible homes, largely in the starboard quarterberth. As Matt and I finally crawl into our bunks in the dark of night we hear Ben still on deck, tending to some B-list rigging details. *Snow Petrel* gently rolls in the placid Southern Ocean swells which have sneaked into the channel and wrapped their way into the bay. We are ready at last.

We were about to get seriously under-way, four days after our declared deadline – a deadline which had been set bearing in mind that we could not safely remain in Antarctica beyond the beginning of February. If the trip down was to take three weeks, this would allow less than a week for exploration.

However, as Ben had pointed out, the voyage might achieve only one goal: namely to view an iceberg. So when New Year's day had dawned with a three day storm warning, we simply heaved a sigh and began the B-list. We all prefer placid departures.

5 JANUARY
0545 HRS

I wake early and fire up the stove for a cup of tea. It is partly a ritual of habit, and partly a self-appointed task associated with my novel role as cabin-boy. Somehow, from my many days in the mountains and bush-huts of various

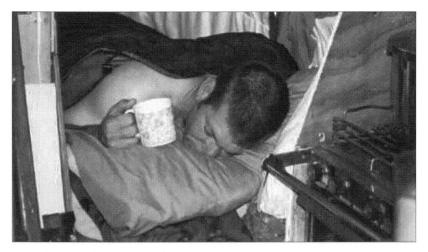

Ben, asleep in the radio cave, often needed some coaxing to wake up

former lives, I have found that the whistling kettle defines the start of a new day and has a part in establishing its morale.

On deck there is a slight dew and no wind. A steel fishing boat lies on anchor nearby, its crew going about their business of preparing for a day's work. I wave and wonder what they would be thinking if they could know that we weren't just another cruising boat out for a few days' relaxation in the channel.

Ben has replaced all the rigging screws in the night, a job that had been on his mental A-list, but relegated during the prioritising. He lies in his quarterberth, face squashed against the pillow. He has never been a natural early riser, and groggily accepts my cup of tea, grumbling that I have to stop being so cheerful. Matt doesn't drink tea, but accepts a hot chocolate happily enough before we set about the last few jobs whilst discussing the weather forecast, a 20 knot sou'wester. After the storm-force southerlies of the New Year period, we know there'll be some big residual swells out there, but in this quiet little haven it's hard to imagine.

The last job before departure involves re-stowing the two life-rafts and three survival suits so that access will be easier. Then it's time to go. Ben and I unshackle the anchor from its chain and bring it below to lash it among the foc'sle gear. We won't be needing it for a while now, and the weight is better low down and further aft. Not a moment too soon, with the bow beginning to gently lift and plunge as soon as we clear the Southport heads. I glance at the GPS, already programmed to the waypoint of Cape Denison. It reads 1442 nautical miles, or close to three thousand kilometres allowing for the expected tacking. We are seriously under way at last.

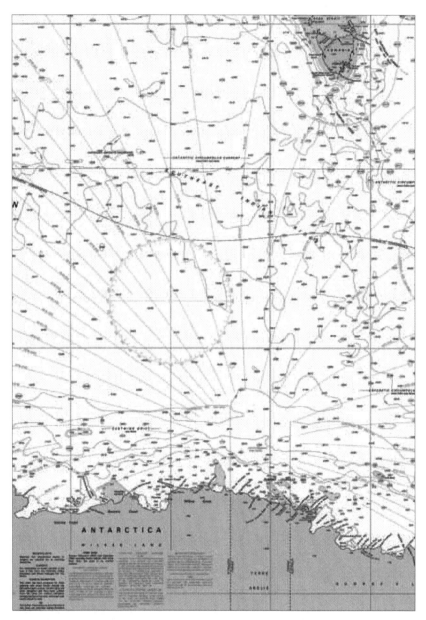

Chart of the Southern Ocean

NOT TO BE USED FOR NAVIGATION
COURTESY OF THE AUSTRALIAN HYDROGRAPHIC SERVICE (RAN)

PHASE 2

The Roaring Forties

Hobart lies at about 43 South, and Cape Denison is at 67 South. Each degree of latitude is sixty nautical miles, or nearly double that in kilometres. Travelling at our hoped for average of ninety-odd miles per day we hoped to achieve the trip in under three weeks. Given that the first part of our journey lay in the belt of westerlies known as the Roaring Forties and Furious Fifties, we expected to have reaching conditions with the wind somewhere off our beam for the first week. A fast point of sail, although a vulnerable one in big seas. When sailing side-on like this, any breaking sea which is higher than the width of a boat poses the risk of capsizing it onto its beam ends or worse.

5 JANUARY
1200 HRS

Astern lies land, low on the horizon. Bruny Island has merged with mainland Tasmania. The channel that disgorged us into the Southern Ocean, five hours ago, is no longer recognisable. The 23 knot west-sou'westerly has pushed up a lumpy cross-sea as we tight-reach on a southerly heading.

Snow Petrel is a dreadfully lively little thing. Not a thoroughbred by any stretch. Just a plain enough Roberts 34. Ben has described her as an ocean-going four-wheel drive, and by that he means an army Jeep, not a Subaru. But she has an abrupt motion I'm not used to. Our own ketch, a bigger Herreshoff, would be riding these waves with a more deliberate ease.

As I struggle to rig a shaft brake amid the odour of diesel and engine oil I can feel the bile rising in my throat.

This can't be true. I don't get sea-sick. We're all immune to that land-lubber's curse. Out in the cockpit I glance at my sons. Ben is on top of the world. All his plans are finally coming to fruition. He's wearing a cheeky grin and practising using the dodger dome. Matt's looking decidedly pale though and has a stupid half-grin on his face as he lolls with suspicious inertness in the lee side of the dodger.

In truth this isn't the first time I've felt queasy. Diesel is the worst culprit. In this case it's more the unfamiliar motion and I'm a little relieved to note Matt's discomfort. It will pass after a day or two. Meanwhile there are watches to keep and a boat to keep sailing.

To our south-east lies the rocky islet of Pedra Branca, and Ben cheerfully announces that he's altering course to sail past at close quarters as our final salute to land for a week or three. Splashes begin to slop into the cockpit as our angle changes, but the motion eases correspondingly. Matt is the first to notice a pod of dolphins racing alongside, and is immediately up in the rigging with his new video camera. It's precariously wet for him, perched on the ratlines, and I can't stop myself growling at him for risking his new purchase so soon in the voyage instead of protecting it for the chance of far more spectacular footage in southern latitudes. Dolphins are always a thrill, but they're certainly not a rare sight.

It's a parental habit I guess, to criticise the decisions or risks taken by one's children. I bite my tongue and leave him to it. After all he bought it with his own precious money and then had to put up with all our criticism for frittering his savings on such an impractical purchase. But it would be such a pity to ruin a brand new camcorder so soon in the voyage …

Yacht design is a subject that invokes strong opinions. Only one point about it reaches universal agreement: namely that there is no such thing as a perfect boat. To achieve speed you sacrifice comfort. Cruising boats tend to be heavier displacement than racing boats, with a slower more deliberate motion.

One of our younger sons, Sam, has a marine technology degree and is committed to designing for speed. Meanwhile Ben has a Nautical Science diploma and is vehemently outspoken on issues of seaworthiness in design. Sparks fly when they face off on the technicalities of wetted surface and hull sections.

The simplest backyard built boats are hard-chine, with slab sides and vee bottoms. It makes them easy to build but can compromise their

A contrast in hull shapes: *Snow Petrel* and *New Zealand Maid* show off their bottoms

motion in a beam sea. I was brought up sailing a hard-chine boat, a 1920s straight stemmer with a long bowsprit, and learned to live with the lurch and snap as each wave picked up the windward chine while the leeward chine simultaneously dropped into a trough.

Then came New Zealand Maid *with her gloriously soft rolling motion. By the mid nineties when Barbara and I took up tuna trolling in the Tasman Sea on the hard-chined fishing ketch* Sunniva, *we had to get used to the vicious lurch all over again.* Snow Petrel *is a backyard builder's compromise design, double-chine with three plates per side. Once again our bodies had some reprogramming to do.*

In the early seventies the IOR racing rules began to affect yacht design. To cheat the rules the designers pinched the ends. With little buoyancy in the bow and stern these yachts suffered the vice of hobby-horsing – burying their noses deep into each approaching sea and pivoting on their fat midships section like a floating see-saw. Unfortunately for Snow Petrel, *Bruce Roberts designed her to look like a racy IOR yacht. Not as extreme but still prone to deep pitching.*

On the positive side though, we didn't have to suffer the bone-jarring pounding of a modern flat sectioned planing yacht. And with over a ton of provisions and fuel aboard, the extra displacement may have helped.

Our last sight of land. The rocky islet of Pedra Branca is like an apartment block for wildlife

1330 HRS

Pedra Branca is now abeam, little more than a giant cliff-sided rock, sixty-odd metres tall and two or three hundred metres long with a saddle separating two peaks. It is more white than grey, the excrement from more than ten thousand seabirds – mostly gannets and albatrosses – whitewashing its slab sides in long vertical streaks which contrast sharply against the horizontal layers weathered into the rock surfaces.

We sail a mere quarter mile away, down the lee eastern side. The place is like a giant apartment block for birds, with hundreds of fur seals hauled out on the ground floor. A few miles to the east a tall narrow rock rises sheer out of the sea, its resemblance to a lighthouse earning it the name Eddystone.

Around us are hundreds of shearwaters diving continuously on the same schools of fish that Matt's dolphins are herding. Despite my queasiness I'm drinking in the scene. In an era of diminishing species it's a comfort to see such a teeming multitude of seemingly undisturbed wildlife.

Ben heads down below to plot a course clear of the foul ground to the south of the islet. Matt has already taken his cameras down and is now settling uncomfortably in the cockpit. With the last landmark falling away behind us, the distance ahead is sinking in.

'Welcome to three weeks of hell,' grins Ben.

There is a marked difference in wave patterns between coastal and offshore sailing. Many factors are involved, including wind influences, wave reflection or refraction, tidal currents and depth of water.

Fishermen and sailors often refer to 'the shelf'. The continental shelf they mean – inside it or outside it. There's a big difference in wave patterns. Sydney-Hobart sailors stay inside to maximise the East Australian current but when the Southerly busters hit, the canny sailors go outside. They know very well that strong wind acting against a current creates vicious steep-fronted seas.

Some of Australia's nastiest freak waves occur in the vicinity of Bass Strait between Tasmania and the mainland. Many pundits credit this to the rapidly shoaling waters tripping up the ocean swells. There's a simple enough formula relating to the height (and corresponding root) of a wave and the depth of water. If the root reaches the sea-bottom, the wave will rear up like a giant surf break.

Ben has seen two so-called freak waves from the bridges of ships. One, in the Australian Bight, makes my hair stand on end whenever I think of his description. He looked out to starboard and only fifty metres away was a chasm. A twenty metre deep slab-sided 'hole' in the sea, rushing past at the speed of a wave. And on its rear wall the water appeared to rush 'up-hill'.

To the south of Tasmania the shelf stretches a hundred-odd miles and is studded with undersea peaks. The local fishermen talk of a three knot sub-surface current of denser water. To a wave, this is as good as a shallow bottom. The area is notorious. You won't find any fishermen there in a blow.

1800 HRS

I'm angry with my body. So often on past trips I've watched with slightly smug sympathy as fellow crew retch miserably in the scuppers. And now the boot's on the other foot. Ben kindly pretends not to notice as my reflux spasm finally opens a floodgate. I feel a fraud, a failure. Matt has turned noticeably paler at the sound of my disgrace.

Ben has handpicked a crew supposedly immune to such lubberly weakness and I've let him down. I know it'll pass, and I know that this isn't enough to stop me carrying out my key watch-keeping duties, but I feel cheated. I'm being robbed of the full enjoyment of what should be an ultimate leave-taking of land. Here we are, sailing due south on the voyage of a lifetime and instead of relishing it, I'm huddled in the corner of the cockpit, conserving my energy and limiting my food intake to water, bananas and crackers. Even so, I still don't bother with seasick pills. I know it will run its course soon enough.

At least we're making good progress. At a steady six knots on the GPS we should be off the shelf tomorrow morning. The sou'wester is veering to the west and has freshened to 28 knots. The seas are approaching from two angles and accentuating the motion. Ben and Matt slab a second reef in the main as the evening darkens, and we move into watch-keeping routines.

Watch-keeping duties rule a sailor's life on passage. Every skipper has his own preferences when setting up a watch routine. On ships the convention is three four-hour watches every twelve hours. But on yachts there are many constraints. I've tried all sorts of combinations on previous voyages. Four hours is a tediously long time in a cold open cockpit continuously helming. I prefer three hours. In nasty stuff we have often contracted the watches to two or less. The downside of a short watch is the correspondingly short off-watch.

Of course when there are plenty of crew to share around this isn't a problem. It's even better when there's a self-steering unit like Ben's Sooty, to relieve the tyranny of the helm. For this trip, Ben had opted for two hours on and four off. Single watches. The first two hours off after each person's watch would be a standby period, so he could be called up if necessary. But where possible, any sail change or reefing should be delayed until the watch change, when two are on deck in their gear.

The timing of these watches would allow Ben to do radio scheds during his evening watch. Meals were left out of the equation except dinner, when we would all be around. It has always been a ritual on our family voyages to have a happy hour before dinner, a chance to come together and enjoy each other's company once each day.

2100 HRS

Sched time. Our first radio contact since we've left land. Ben bought his HF marine set second hand for $100 not long before we left, and mounted it deep inside his quarter-berth – the driest place in the boat, he'd claimed.

That means he has to wriggle headfirst into a rectangular tunnel-like bunk space to do the radio scheds. Rather antisocial, but it works. This evening I've decided to name it the 'radio cave', and despite our queasiness Matt and I are hovering around the companionway to listen to the coms.

I'm a bit sceptical about this cheap radio, and it's nice to have the sat-phone that Don and Margie McIntyre loaned us unexpectedly not long before we left. It gives an alternative, if expensive, means of contacting the outside world.

For so many years I've been the one doing radio coms, and it's a humbling experience for me to be a mere cabin-boy listening to a skipper on that handpiece. A yacht's radio voice is its mouthpiece. Its very identity is linked to that voice. *Snow Petrel* tonight has become Ben himself to any ears out there.

Tonight on four megs we have bingo! Mike Harris, our good friend live-aboard neighbour and electronics guru booms in, his broad English vowels contrasting with Ben's short Kiwi ones. With my eyes closed I can picture Mike at the chart table of his home-built *Pangolin 2*, probably manipulating the laptop screen as he talks. He's found a great website, he tells Ben after noting our position and speed. It's called the 'Grib Files', predicting wind speed and direction for any bit of ocean for up to a week ahead. Apparently it's already told him correctly what we now have, and the good news is that there's nothing sinister out there for us for a while, just two days of twenty to thirty knot westerlies.

He signs off after a short chat and, with barely a hesitation, Barbara's voice fills the cabin. I'm stunned. When we left yesterday, *New Zealand Maid*'s radio didn't seem to be working at all, and there was no time to fix it. She's spent all day stripping down all the vital wiring and remounting the aerial connections. It's certainly worked and her signal's as strong as Mike's. She's done her own homework on the weather too and can confirm from the Buoyweather website what Mike has relayed us. Ben asks her to stand by and wriggles out of the cave so that I can slide in on my sensitive stomach for a quick chat. It can't be too long as the batteries are taking a hammering.

Barbara has overheard Ben hinting to Mike that his crew's a bit under the weather and I can hear the incredulity in her voice as she quizzes me in an embarrassingly loud voice. It's hard to keep secrets on the airwaves and you can't whisper, so I come clean and reassure her that it's a mere touch of queasiness, nothing too serious. The motion's so lively, I explain, but I'll come right tomorrow.

There are other ears out there too. As soon as she signs off there are good luck calls from three other boats, all good friends. My humiliation is complete. I slink off to my bunk for the remaining two hours of my watch off.

This was to be the first significant voyage that I had done without Barbara. And six weeks would be the longest period in our thirty four year marriage

*that we would have been continuously apart. That is, of course, if this voyage
was to run its course as planned.*

*So to have an etheric umbilical cord like this was significant for both
of us. And it was a relief to have heard her sounding so confident and happy
on the air – just a pity she had to talk so loud ...*

2145 HRS

The motion in my bunk is cradle-like. Lying prone like this I don't feel
the plunge and snap of each wave, and my stomach relaxes. On the deck
directly above me I can hear the tramp of Ben's feet and the zip of his
harness clip on the safety line as he does his rounds to the foredeck. He's
constantly watchful, checking for tell tale signs of rig weakness or chafe,
checking the set of the partly rolled genoa and inspecting lashings on the
spinnaker pole.

He seems impervious to the motion and I'm pleased for him. It's a
strange feeling to have reversed roles with my own son. At this instant I'm the
weak one and he's emanating that supreme invincibility that a child expects in
a parent. I think back to his birth, to that tiny six pound wrinkled specimen of
humanity, helpless and so full of potential. He was always such an ambitiously
active little baby. Bursting undercooked into the world ten days early, he was
crawling at four months and walking by his tenth. It's a miracle he survived
his first five years.

I hear Ben come below for Matt. There are the sounds of feet and
winches, and I know they must be slabbing in a third reef. Then the rustle of
wet weather gear being removed and comparative silence, marred only by the
squeaks and groans of a yacht under way, and later the sound of Matt retching
in his solitude.

*The Roaring Forties have been our stamping ground since the boys
were born. And Barbara's and mine before that. I remember as a child
reconciling myself to the terror of rising and falling on grey-green waves
in the knowledge of great depths extending far below, far deeper than my
small body could ever survive. And I recall a distinct moment, a flash of
conscious realisation that buoyancy would overcome each wave – that I
could trust the flimsy vessel to carry me safely through the short voyage.
In that instant, at the age of nine, I gained the confidence to weather a
thousand perils at sea.*

*I remember Ben in the cockpit of his grandparents' ketch on a crossing
of Tasman Bay. He was bellowing in terror as only a two-year-old can, as*

we braved the swells. At what point in his formative years did he experience the epiphany of buoyancy? At quite a young age, I suspect. For Matt I have no recollection of any obvious nervousness. Perhaps he absorbed an ocean's worth of confidence by osmosis, passed on telepathically from four older brothers and a pair of parents all at home in the environment and enjoying the sensation of the elements.

6 JANUARY
1200 HRS

Midday, and I'm back on watch for the third time since last night's sched. It feels like a ghost ship in many ways, with each of us making only brief contact during the changeover. The skies have cleared and Ben has shaken out the third reef at the 1000 hr changeover with Matt. After the thirty knot overnight westerly, it seems the Front has gone through and it has eased to a more pleasant twenty knots. The seas are settling into a more predictable pattern today, without the overlay of yesterday's sou'westerly cross sea. But the big ocean swell under the surface waves is still there, betraying wind somewhere down in the deep Southern Ocean.

I'm settling down too, on a diet of easy stuff and a deliberate economy of movement. The idea is to suppress that dreaded uncontrollable vomit spasm for long enough for my body to re-programme. It's slowly working.

Ben has logged our day's run at 132 miles. Whoopee, at this speed we'll be there in no time!

7 JANUARY
0100 HRS

The night watches are the loneliest. I'm sitting out here in the shelter of the dodger listening to the waves thumping the hull and hissing past. We're back down to triple reefed main with most of the genoa rolled away. It has risen to a near gale, gusting around 35 knots.

Sooty's doing a great job. I think back to our passages in the old days, sitting alone and exposed behind the wheel on the *Maid*, with a line tied to my wrist and the other end to Barbara's ankle as she slept below. The kids were all small back then, on those three day east coast passages home to Napier from the South Island. At seven years of age, Ben was already determined to do his stints on the helm and we'd sometimes let him do half hour day-watches while one of us stayed handy.

Memories fill my watch, and I find myself becoming increasingly at home in this capsule of steel. *Snow Petrel*'s hull has a different ring from the *Maid*'s, and her alloy mast makes a tinging noise with the slap of a halyard, so different from the dull clonk of our own wooden masts.

These two hour watches are great. It's already time to call Ben, but I delay for an extra ten minutes to let him sleep. I'm fine here just now and he could do with a bit of extra sleep. Would I do this if he wasn't my son? I'm not sure. Somehow I feel a wave of affection for them all.

Snow Petrel *was designed as a mast-head sloop. That means she has two key working sails, a main behind the mast and a genoa ahead of it. Both sails are pulled up right to the top of the mast. Ben has installed a babystay for this trip and turned her into a temporary cutter with two heads'ls. The much smaller stays'l between the genoa and mast doubles as a storm heads'l. She's not a true cutter because her unrolled genoa is much larger than a cutter's yankee jib. We term it a slutter rig – neither fish nor fowl.*

There are sound reasons for the modification. Firstly the extra forestay adds an element of safety. Forestays have been known to break and the extra support gives peace of mind. In a race around the buoys it would be a damn nuisance, interfering with the genoa during every tack, but on this voyage we would seldom be tacking. And after we roll the genoa right away, the snug balanced sail plan of a triple reefed main and stays'l is a safe one.

The roller reefing option on the powerful genoa is a fantastic option. Without it we would need to brave the foredeck for fifteen minutes or more, each time we changed between four different heads'ls. Wet and dangerous work. On the Maid *I often avoid changing heads'ls until it's blatantly necessary. It's a job that saps my energy and I'm inherently lazy. Of course then I curse myself. In a rising wind the sail change will have become even more difficult.*

On Snow Petrel *the roller furler allows us to change down with the flick or two of a wrist. It simply rolls up like a giant vertical window blind. Two rolls is the equivalent of changing from number one to number two heads'l. And it can be done on a two-speed winch in half a minute from the comfort of the dodger. As for the stays'l, it will generally be up all the time unless we are lucky enough to have a moderate tail wind.*

To tame the mains'l, the slab reefing system is relatively painless. True we have to go forward to the mast to work the two winches but that's no big drama with a sail this modest in size. It's generally a one man job.

Each of the three reef points takes a sizable slab out of the main. And if
we need anything smaller, there's the tiny orange storm trys'l with its own
independent mast track.

1140 HRS

KaBOOM! What a way to wake up. I feel *Snow Petrel* being pile-driven
sideways for at least twenty metres. But we've stayed fairly upright. Matt's
on watch and I stick my head up in the dome of the closed hatch to see him
slouched happily enough in the shelter of the dodger. The beam seas are
whitecapped and fairly steep but not high enough to be alarming. Getting
the odd slammer like that is just the one in a hundred chance of being in the
exact spot where a wave decides to break. It's like being inside a nine ton steel
bodyboard sideways-on to the surf.

It's nearly my watch anyway, so I grab some lunch before getting my
gear on. The GPS shows us at nearly 48 South. That's further south than
Stewart Island and we are now further south than I've ever sailed before. Ben
has been round Cape Horn twice on big ships but even for him this is the
deepest he's gone under sail. I think back to a midwinter delivery we once
did up the New Zealand west coast. There was snow to sea-level in Milford
Sound, and we were colder then at 44 South in a fifty knot offshore gale than
we are now. But that will change soon enough.

Outside we're trucking along comfortably enough at over five knots,
well reefed down. The swells have picked up to about four metres from the
sou'west, and occasionally during my watch another big sea slams us with
a solid very noisy thump. The wind's back in the west at about thirty knots,
but the cloud's building to the sou'west and I guess there'll be another Front
through later. If these seas keep building, we'll need to angle away to the east
more and take them on the aft quarter. But meantime we're tracking straight
down the rhumb line and making good progress. It's good to be feeling well
again and I'm looking forward to a decent meal this evening.

The last half hour of my watch is back to hand-steering. Sooty has lost
a shackle-pin and wants a rest. I don't bother calling Ben up early. We can fix
it during the watch change. It's strange to be on a tiller again. We've become
complacently dependent on the self-steering soft option. Sooty is as valuable
as two extra crew.

I don't bother sleeping during my standby. It's starting to rain but we're
determined to have our first happy hour at the 1600 hr watch change, tucked
in to the shelter of the dodger together, sharing a can of beer between the three
of us and a packet of chippies.

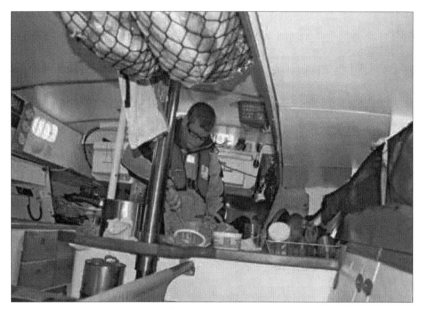

Matt's other favourite place was the galley

The wind eases with the rain and Matt begins enthusiastically cooking up a big pot of bolognaise. I don't know where he learned to love cooking. Certainly not from me! I'm happy to be chief dish-washer on this voyage and leave the culinary expertise to Matt. He's fully over the sensitive tummy stuff too and is tossing herbs and garlic into the pressure cooker like a professional while I stop things sliding off the bench.

It's a great feed. 'The barefoot chef' we nickname him, and award him a ten.

We've always found the pressure cooker great value on passage. When the lid's clamped on tight, its contents are secure. And once it's up to steam, it can be turned off and left to cook without gas.

Snow Petrel, like all sensible voyaging yachts, had a gimballed stove which swung freely as the boat heeled, always staying more or less level. The galley bench had fiddles around it to stop things sliding off. Theoretically. In practice whenever the boat lurched, the cooking bowl or cutting-board would accelerate towards the fiddles and come to an abrupt halt, catapulting the contents towards the chart table.

Matt picked up another useful habit from experience in the galley – he always wore his bib-front over-trousers while cooking in a seaway. It saved him from a scalding or two. Don't know about the bare feet though ...

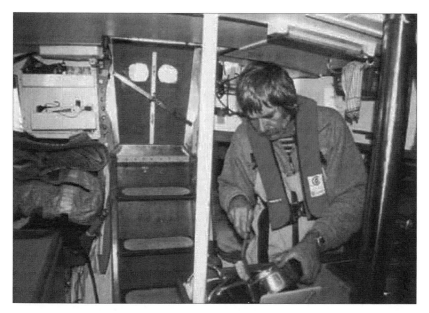

As the cabin boy, I became chief dish-washer. Neither of the boys would eat my cooking!

8 JANUARY
0100 HRS

I've just come on watch, and a half moon is poking its head out of some clearing cloud layers. We're fairly close-hauled now and bashing into a lumpy head-sea. Ben was on watch when the Front came through with a rainsquall and wind shift to the sou'west. He was nearly caught out, uncharacteristically, as the wind had dropped away for a while and he was about to shake out the second reef.

It's already easing back from 30 to 20 knots and I'm enjoying a light show in the sky to the south. It's our first Aurora of the trip, not as spectacular as a couple I've watched in Tasmania, but an exciting reminder of where we're heading. It's frustrating sailing now though. With the wind shift we've had to alter course slightly off the rhumb line, and being close-hauled bashing into a lumpy head sea, our speed is down to four knots. Slow compared to the six we were doing on my last watch.

We've just passed the 49th parallel. I'm doing the maths in my head to pass the time. At four knots heading nearly south, it'll take another 15 hours to get to 50 South. But if we could get back up to six again we'd be there by late morning. At least the barometer's rising.

I don't know why, but the midnight watch always seems the longest.

Midnight sunset in Antarctic Treaty waters

PHASE 3

The Furious Fifties and Screaming Sixties

There is something intensely private about a small boat passage. It takes several days for the personal contraction to occur, but it can become quite addictive. After a long passage we have often had difficulty adjusting back to the real world.

Our longest period out of sight of land on the Maid *was five weeks. Landing in a foreign port with people and traffic was rather like emerging into bright light from a tunnel. Dazzling and almost frightening.*

The microcosm you inhabit while on passage is more like the inside of a dome than a tunnel. You are constantly in the centre of a disc of sea with a visible horizon radius of about three miles. Above is a dome of blue or grey or speckled black.

Your only habitable area is little larger than a walk-in wardrobe. Your only company is more often asleep than awake during your conscious hours. And yet you are free of the constraints of everyday society. Your existence has been stripped to its barest essentials. Your sleep patterns are re-programmed into short blocks, irrespective of the passage of the sun. You become introverted and focused on a few vital specifics. Food, scheds, progress reports and weather predictions dominate your thoughts.

But it is not a prison. You are free to leave whenever you wish. That is why a supply of engrossing books is vital on a well prepared yacht. A good book will whisk you away to another time and place.

8 JANUARY
1418 HRS

I've come off my midday watch and am doing the countdown on the GPS. While I wait, I'm decorating the whiteboard with a message for the others. It's a series of road signs. 'WELCOME TO THE FURIOUS FIFTIES' reads the big one, footnoted 'proceed with caution'. A smaller one reads 'THE ROARING FORTIES FAREWELLS YOU – thank you for sailing carefully.'

I glance at the GPS again. Three seconds of latitude to go. Time to add a couple more signs – diamond shaped road warnings. 'Beware strong winds' and 'Whales crossing'.

Three, two, one – whoopee. Fifty South! We celebrate with an early happy hour. Again a can of beer – shared between the three of us, to Matt's disgust – with a plate of crackers and gherkins. The wind is veering to the west and we're up to five knots again.

Ben boots up the weather fax at the end of his watch. There's a deep Low to our west tracking this way. It'll be interesting to hear what Mike's predicting for us on tonight's sched.

Ben's weather fax was just a cheap $200 laptop hooked into the headphone jack on the radio. We'd used this setup on the Maid *for years and it was a fraction of the cost of a dedicated fax. Of course there was no hard copy, he just saved the image onto the hard drive.*

This was very much a budget cruise. It would be easy to spend a fortune on gear for a trip like this, except none of us had a fortune at the time. The one thing Ben agonised over was whether to buy a radar. In fog, with ice around, it would be a very helpful extra lookout. But then he blew his tiny budget on a new propeller shaft assembly and the decision was made for him.

9 JANUARY
0015 HRS

So much for the Furious Fifties. We've run out of wind. It's a clear moonlit night and we've had full sail up since Matt's chilli con carne dinner. But the sched was a bit sobering. Mike was booming in as normal, and talked at length about the possible track of the Low which is approaching from the west. It's a deep one of 985 millibars, and is moving fast. If it curves to the north of us and we move fast enough then we may escape the worst of its power. But if it keeps tracking straight we could cop it tomorrow afternoon.

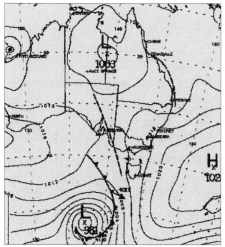

Detail of weather fax, 9 January, 0000 hrs
COURTESY OF THE AUSTRALIAN BUREAU OF METEOROLOGY

Ben reads the weather fax from the entrance to his cave

We're wallowing around now while the sails flap and chafe. It's time to fire up the engine and sheet in. Running the engine will help the batteries, and maybe we'll get ourselves into its safer southern quadrant if we move faster. Ben emerges almost immediately – it's dreadfully noisy in his radio cave berth. He helps me set up the unfamiliar electric tiller pilot before shifting into my bunk away from the engine.

'Sweep' is his nickname for this tiller-pilot. When he was little, Sooty and Sweep were two of his favourite TV cartoon characters so he's passed the names on to these little crew members. He tells me that the sound of Sooty's squeaky rope-blocks conjures up memories of the characters' voices.

I see out the rest of my watch to a moonlit sea and the drone of an engine.

The science of meteorology has been described as a black art. It's the closest humanity has come to successful crystal ball gazing. Computer models now can do amazing things in predicting the eddies and interactions between various layers in the atmosphere.

But there are still too many variables to allow total accuracy. We were once on passage back to New Zealand from Noumea when a tropical Low spawned in the North Tasman Sea. Neither the American nor French seven day models we had studied three days earlier had predicted this unfortunate turn of events. And we were at the mercy of its track. Sure we had our trusty laptop weather fax to consult, but with the Australian fax predicting the low centre to pass north of us, and the Kiwi fax showing it curving south, there was nothing we could do except batten down and sit it out. Like sailors of old, we turned to the trusty barometer as our most useful tool.

1415 HRS

What a change there's been over the past few hours. The barometer has been dropping like a stone – from 1010 to 991 since midnight. Ben managed to complete two more B-list jobs during the morning: sealing up a leak around the rudder stock and splicing up a warp for the drogue – a drag device we can stream aft to help control our direction if it gets really nasty.

Matt's been cooking up a huge casserole while it's not too rough, though *Snow Petrel* is already starting to corkscrew with one set of waves catching her under her aft quarter while another rapidly building set is coming in on our beam.

Ben's most recent fax shows the Low centre almost right on top of us. We dumped the main completely on my midday watch and are now broad reaching under storm stays'l with only a scrap of genoa left unrolled. It's 45 knots out there already.

I'm resting in my sleeping bag for now, stripped to my thermals, while Matt opens up the pressure cooker to check if it's ready. It's a huge pot of stew, enough for three days of bad weather – a lesson he's learned from his mum – and a delicious aroma fills the cabin. He calls Ben down to grab a feed while the going's good. Then, suddenly, our world comes unstuck.

I'm enveloped in a roar of noise, and gravity has strangely reversed. From my vantage point, pinned between the locker doors and the deck-head, I'm aware of being inside a waterfall. From the skylight and ventilators on the cabin-top I'm being squirted with water like a fire hydrant. I see Ben jammed in the open companionway door, one leg in and one still out. He is enveloped in a torrent of rushing water, his body stemming the flow of what otherwise would be an open sluice-gate. Meanwhile Matt is laughing hysterically, pinned against the galley cabin-side at the mercy of a still hot stove-top and a deluge of white water.

The sensation lasts long enough to register the sense of motion. We are moving sideways, very quickly. In fact *Snow Petrel* has become like a giant water-scoop, mast underwater, keel out, being driven sideways at twenty-odd knots for fifty or sixty metres. Her deck is like the blade of a great bulldozer pushing water. Small wonder the supposedly watertight skylight is gushing all over me.

Snow Petrel's log simply reads: 'Took a big sea. Broached. Ben in hatchway. Shipped water. Stew everywhere.' Another entry, ninety minutes later, reveals the extent of the inconvenience: 'Still cleaning up. What a mess. Food everywhere. Beds soaked.' But the reality was that we'd got off lightly. A knockdown like this puts an enormous strain on both the hull and its rig. We could easily have rolled right over.

Ben was embarrassed to have been caught out with the hatch open. But Matt and I have been caught off-guard ourselves on other occasions. Often the worst seas rear up out of the blue, the product of two converging waves that come together in a sudden explosion of white water.

In flippant terms, this broach was nature's way of telling us to slow down and alter course. To broach is to be overpowered by a quartering sea so that the rudder can no longer keep a vessel on its course. In an instant it will slew around in a giant foaming skid until it is side-on to a breaking wave. The rest is up to the gods.

2130 HRS

We're pretty much cleaned up now and Matt managed to salvage enough stew from the back of the food lockers for a reasonable feed. The bilges are dry again and the electrics have survived. We're going to have to live with wet mattresses and sleeping bags for a while, but things could be a lot worse.

It's shrieking out there, between 50 and 60 knots maybe. The sea is a mass of foam with long streaks between each crest. We're doing watches mostly inside with our heads in the hatch dome and hanging on tight. But the motion has become lazier now that the drogue is out. *Snow Petrel* has a slightly laboured feel, akin to a fishing boat towing a trawl net. She feels much more controlled. It's a Seabrake plastic cone back there, a hundred metres behind us, weighed down with fathoms of chain.

The fax tonight looked a horror show, as if we're in the middle of a bullseye of isobar lines, so close together that they seem almost solid. But the barometer seems to have bottomed out and the wind has rapidly backed from north to west with a patch of blue showing briefly overhead. From now on things should steadily get better. Mike's forecast predicts a better day tomorrow, and Barbara came up on the sched too, taking the news of our knockdown calmly enough. Ben played down the drama in his description, but Barbara has had enough time in heavy weather to read between the lines of his carefully worded description.

Sleep doesn't come easily in my off-watch. It's not the motion or even the unremitting racket. And I've got used to my wet sleeping bag. No, it's these bloody stupid bike helmets that Ben's insisted on us all wearing, even in bed, while there's a knockdown risk. I'm getting a crick in my neck.

There are two other interesting aspects of Southern Ocean weather worth mentioning. One involves the density of air, and has stuck in my mind ever since I heard Peter Blake talking about it. A gale in the tropics has noticeably less pressure in its warm air flow than an equal wind speed in cold latitudes. Denser cold air has more solidity about it. From a sailor's viewpoint this equates to pressure on the sails which affect heeling and reefing issues. From a meteorologist's viewpoint it is probably reflected in the properties of waves, which are essentially the interface of two fluid mediums – air and water.

The second fact, which I learned from Ben on this voyage, relates to energy and spin. The vortices we see as low pressure systems are influenced by the coriolis effect – the spin that causes bathwater to spiral. The internal energy varies with latitude, just as the earth's surface speed varies between equator and polar regions. There is a complex interplay between coriolis and the internal centrifugal forces. As a result the speed of air flowing from high to low pressure systems will vary depending on one's latitude.

Many enthusiasts measure the interval between isobars on their fax to estimate likely wind-speeds. I've done it for years in New Zealand – there's a formula. But as Snow Petrel *was progressing deeper into the high latitudes, the ratio was steadily changing. Ben had even found a sliding scale to help.*

The result is that the close spacings of isobars around our Low generated us a mere sixty knots, whereas the same spacings in the mid tropics would maybe generate a hundred. Curious. They say that when you stop learning you die.

10 JANUARY
1200 HRS

Mike's predictions were correct and we're now bowling along in a mere thirty knots under trysail and even a scrap of genoa. *Snow Petrel* loved us when we hauled in the drogue an hour ago . She positively shook herself and kicked up her heels at the sense of freedom. She was labouring like a filly hauling a dray all night. But it was for her own good. And ours of course.

The noon to noon run was a mere 66 miles compared with an average of 120 over the previous three. In fact the VMG was even worse, as we were 30 degrees off course. Still, better late than never and no-one's complaining. There are still some pretty big beam seas and Ben's being cautious keeping our speed down. The latest fax shows another deep Low heading this way after a day of lighter winds.

It's nice to see the sun breaking through the clouds during my watch but we're really starting to notice the cold now, at nearly 53 South. We're expecting to be halfway some time tomorrow, and Matt's already planning a party of sorts. Half-way parties have always been a big tradition on our voyages and it's the first time Barbara hasn't been around to organise one. As self-appointed ship's cook, Matt plans to do his mum proud.

During the busy weeks before our departure Barbara was busily sewing for us. It was only one of a number of her default roles, and at this point in the voyage we were really appreciating some of her tangible work. She'd bought metres of polar-fleece and sewn us all fluffy warm sleeping bag liners and fleecy pants. There was plenty else to sew too. Lee-cloths for the bunks, spray-cloths for the cockpit, storage nets and a dozen little extras. At the same time, she was cooking for us, mentoring, advising, and bipartisanly listening to our little grumps and grizzles about each other. She assembled the most comprehensive first aid kit I've ever seen, combining New Zealand Maid's *category one offshore kit with Ben's kit and various donated extras from some generous medical friends.*

Probably her most valuable gift was her advice. All the stuff I've left her to deal with in the past while I've been focused on rigging and navigation. Things like hygiene issues, provisioning options, food storage and preparation. All her experience in nurturing a whole family through difficult voyages was poured out whenever we were together for breathers or meals. And as we now entered the coldest phase of the voyage, we were often to remember her advice.

11 JANUARY
1230 HRS

It's a special day today and even the sun is out to help us celebrate. There's a steady 17 knot nor'westerly and we're rollicking along under full sail. But it's cold, markedly colder even than yesterday. There are a lot more birds around today, clouds of petrels and shearwaters – quite a crowd compared with the infrequent albatrosses we've been seeing further north, and there's some unusual cumulus on the horizon too. Ben's convinced that we've crossed the convergence this morning, the distinct transition line between cold Antarctic waters and the merely cool waters further north. To prove it he runs the thermometer under the galley seawater tap. It reads only five degrees compared with eight yesterday.

That gives us two reasons for a celebration. Three if you count the first fine day of the trip. We've decided to set the half way point at 711 nautical miles to Cape Denison. That's half of the 1422 miles we had to go when we left the anchorage at Southport. We're expecting to get there at around 1400 hrs and Matt already has a chocolate cake in the oven.

How he still manages to cook in bare feet I don't know. True when I was younger I wore bare feet everywhere, even in frosts, but it was a hippy thing and now I suffer the consequences. To make up for the poor circulation I've been wearing either my ugboots or seaboots whenever I'm out of my bunk. It's my watch so I'm popping up and down like a yoyo. I accidentally stand on his bare toes while I'm licking the cake bowl. His slightly grumpy response is ludicrously self-controlled: 'I'd *appreciate* it if you wouldn't stand on my foot Dad'. I'll swear we have the politest cook in the Southern Ocean.

The cake comes out all heaped up in a corner of the cake dish like a sloping wave. The oven must have been unbalanced in its gimbals. Matt's not worried. He's got an idea.

An hour or so later we have countdown. Just as well, because I'm hungry. Matt's cake is a masterpiece. Despite being a family of five boys they all love wacky cake decorating. It dates back to the school competitions years ago when we lived in a country school-house. This one's right up there with the best of them. It's become a landscape sloping down to the sea and iced in white. True to the chart of Cape Denison, it has a boat harbour of blue scalloped out of it, with a red jellybean boat securely anchored. On the shoreline is a convincing chocolate Mawson's Hut, and the whole landscape is littered with little black and white jellybean penguins. 'Cake Denison', he proclaims triumphantly, and we bargain over which parts of the landscape to eat first.

As this is a really special occasion we share two beer cans between us to wash it down, then move on to a delicious bacon and egg fry-up. The only thing to mar the occasion is the speed with which the barometer is dropping.

At latitude 55 South we were now effectively out of reach of any easy rescue. It was a long way to the nearest naval base and we had to be self-sufficient. With a water temperature this low even our two liferafts would be very cold little escape pods. Prudent sailing and a jury rig if necessary, would be the best way to get home.

Put in perspective, three of Australia's most famous Southern Ocean rescues took place in latitudes well to our north. Isabelle Autessier in 1995 was rescued at 49 South, while the even greater publicised dual rescues of Thierry Dubois and Tony Bullimore were at 52 South. I remember reading the details at the time and being staggered at the distance which HMAS Adelaide had to steam to get there – 1400 nautical miles from Fremantle, over three days at triple the speed of most cruising yachts. We were definitely on our own and were constantly aware of it, despite our banter.

12 JANUARY
0115 HRS

It's a cold and wet watch tonight. The barometer was 993 millibars on my midday watch and when I came back on at midnight it had plummeted to 974. That's the biggest twelve hour fall I've ever experienced. We're all nervous about what's on the way. Especially as nine of those millibars have dropped in the last four hours.

The rule of thumb I've always used up in the mid latitudes was to expect at least a 35 knot force eight gale if the rate of fall is two per hour. But the weather systems work differently down here and none of us can be sure what's going to happen.

At least this midnight watch isn't dragging like it usually does. My adrenaline is up. Ben and Matt dumped the main completely this afternoon as a precaution and we're now running fast under a partly rolled genoa, with a 35 knot northerly right up our tail. But *Snow Petrel*'s motion is starting to change. I can sense a distinct new set of waves coming in from the beam. It's a sure sign of a big windshift. Either a very tight fast-moving Low, or more likely a Front.

The worst thing about a tail wind is that the rain drives straight into the dodger. Before we left, Barbara sewed us a canvas spray curtain to partly close off the dodger, but it's only secured with a bungy cord and in these circumstances it flaps around a bit.

Suddenly the wind goes light. Our motion immediately changes. Short steep seas are catching us on our beam and we begin a lurching roll. I'm now in a quandary. The genoa is flopping around horribly and needs sheeting in. But I can't afford to risk leaving too much sail out in case the new wind comes in with a vengeance. The safest option is to roll it away completely and sheet in the stays'l to reduce the rolling. Then wait.

I don't have to wait long. What a relief. A nice little westerly, only 20 knots and a clearing sky. It's nice to see the stars and moon again. When Ben comes up, we'll re-set the main.

We had quite a few discussions about high latitude weather patterns during the trip. The biggest debate was whether the speed of a low pressure centre affected the relative speed of the wind around it. Ben thought it would, but I had my doubts. It didn't fit my perception of the meanness of Southern Ocean weather.

The barometer became scarily low!

Put simply, a Low centre is like a spinning top or a bathplug vortex – clockwise in the Southern Hemisphere. It can race across the ocean at 25 knots or more, with winds of maybe 50 knots near the centre spiralling inwards. According to Ben's math that could mean that if the centre was racing past just south of us we could get a combined total of 75 knots, but if we managed to get south of it then its own speed should partly cancel its internal wind-speeds, leaving us a more comfortable 25 knots. To reinforce his argument he pointed out that the isobars were wider to the south.

Ben's a bit of a mad professor, and he suspected that there were more complex factors involved, but I can say that our observations on this trip did seem to indicate that there may be some substance to the theory.

1600 HRS
This weather's a puzzle. I've never experienced anything like it. During the night the barometer went up a couple of notches but since then has been steadily continuing to fall. At 964 now it's the lowest I've ever seen a barometer and it drops every time I tap it.

The wind's back in the north again at 25 knots, which is great sailing, and our noon to noon run of 139 miles was our best yet. Ben pulled down another weather fax this afternoon but it doesn't seem to match what we've got here. There's a six metre northerly swell, but technically we should be getting southerlies. All very puzzling. The drizzle seems to indicate another Front moving in, so maybe there'll be a wind shift later.

2100 HRS

Unbelievable! 960 millibars. The needle is nearly at rock bottom, and points below the bold words STORMY on the barometer. But here we are rollicking along beautifully in a 14 knot westerly under full sail. It's a gorgeous evening and we've just had one of Matt's best dinners yet. I don't know where he learnt to use all those herbs.

While we've been waiting for the sched we've taken bets on the first iceberg latitude. We're at nearly 58 South and 144 East, and surely there must be some icebergs soon. First we need to think of a prize. Naturally Matt thinks of a can of beer, so we make this the prize for the closest guess. But what about the first sighting? It's a time honoured tradition to reward the sharpest eyes. My idea of a blissful prize would be to skip a watch, so it's agreed. I think of a conservative latitude and record it as 61 degrees 20 minutes.

Ben opts for 62 degrees. Way too far south I think, expecting Matt to go furthest north. But no, he guesses 63 and I snort. I'm super confident we'll see one soon. I can already nearly taste the beer.

Watchkeeping is a subject that creates a lot of debate in voyaging circles. The advent of self-steering systems has created the ability to let a vessel hurtle through the ocean at speed without human input. Solo race yachts, capable of planing at speeds in excess of thirty knots, spend a significant portion of their time with no effective lookout. Naturally there are various modern alarms to help overcome the risks. But under international collision regulations these vessels do push the limits ...

There's a verbal convention on ships during the formal handover between watches. 'You have the ship'. On Snow Petrel *there was no such formality, but always a designated person in charge. He may not have been helming but we had to trust him. And at times, as when Matt was cooking or Ben on scheds, we would cover for each other.*

Naturally there was a degree of vigilance necessary in proportion to risk. In shipping lanes, near the coastal fishing grounds or later when there was ice about, someone would be constantly on deck and regularly scanning the oncoming horizon. Outside these areas though we could relax a little, reading in the cockpit or popping up and down every ten minutes or so for a good look around and an occasional rig check. By 60 South we were almost certainly safe from a flying solo race yacht. Maybe a toothfish poacher, or the French icebreaker. Icebergs too maybe.

Once, on our way home from Tonga on the Maid*, we were within VHF range of* Melinda Lee *when she was rammed and sunk by a ship. It was a* *shocking night with torrential rain reducing visibility to a boat length or two. I had our spreader lights blazing to create a glow in the murk around us. That kind of tragedy was sheer bad luck – wrong place, wrong time. Even the best lookout can be helpless in such conditions.*

13 JANUARY
1400 HRS

It's cold. We're trucking along under triple reefed main and half the genoa. Friday the thirteenth so far has been kind to us and the wind isn't too far south of west at 30 knots. A bit of a lumpy sea is running but there have been dolphins racing alongside us at times and a lot of birds – prions, shearwaters and petrels. Albatrosses too, like lumbering B-52s compared with the dainty smaller birds but always a treat to watch, the way they soar for hours without ever flapping their enormous wings.

To liven things up I play a trick on Ben before I drag him out of his cold wet bunk for his watch. Our wet-weather removal sequence after each watch has become as simplified as possible. So our seaboots are always left tucked into our wet weather trousers, ready to be put back on together – fireman style. Today I sneak down and twist his left seaboot so that it faces backwards.

I try to suppress my laughter as I watch him time after time sleepily trying to insert his toe into his heel space, concealed under the folds of his trousers. Finally he decides that he must be putting on the whole trouser-boot package back to front, so he reverses the lot and tries to climb in the wrong way round. Of course this time the other boot is wrong. Seeing me laughing, he cottons on to the joke and spends the next five minutes gleefully setting up Matt's gear for an even more elaborate twist-up.

By around midnight we would be in Antarctic Treaty waters. Essentially the treaty covering the Antarctic continent also covers the seas surrounding it. The sixtieth parallel is usually the demarcation line.

For Ben this would represent a major achievement. He had set several provisional goals: firstly just to get away, then to reach these waters, see an iceberg and reach the pack ice. Anything else would be a bonus.

The Antarctic Treaty was a huge achievement in preserving the continent's resources and keeping it military free. But like all treaties, it is only as effective as the extent to which the signatory nations are prepared to enforce its provisions. The whaling and toothfish plunder are two cases in point. One change for us, curiously, related to our eggs. We had committed to abide by the same conditions as the charter operators – IAATO – in treaty waters. So, like them, we would no longer dispose of egg wastes into the sea.

The reason for this was to minimise the chance of domestic bird viruses reaching the southern bird populations – especially penguins – via the albumin in egg whites and raw shells. It would certainly help remind us that we were somewhere special.

15 JANUARY
0010 HRS

I've re-decorated the whiteboard again. 'WELCOME TO THE SCREAMING SIXTIES – EXTREME CAUTION NEEDED.' Then – 'beware ice', 'slippery when wet', 'poor visibility'. I'm leaving 'whales crossing' on the board too. The others can read it when they come up for their watches.

It's a weird twilit night. There's simply no horizon and everything's a bland grey. The wind has nearly dropped and the sea's going glassy. Without wind there's nothing to gauge our direction except the GPS. So much for the Screaming Sixties. Sultry Sixties more like.

This is the first time I haven't had a trusty compass to steer by. The compass is still there in the hatchway, its little red light glowing, but the card is jammed on South.

I fire up the engine and try steering by the GPS but it's no good. Without any reference point, not even a star, the GPS track shows that I'm curving away to starboard, overcorrecting to port, and achieving little but a succession of letter 'S's.

Maybe the fluxgate compass in the electric tiller pilot will still work. I hook Sweep to the tiller and plug him in. Ha! No show! He's just done a full figure-eight. Time to give up. I kill the engine, roll up the genoa and sheet the main in hard. Nothing to do but get my headtorch and read a book. Sooner or later we'll get some wind.

The South Magnetic Pole is constantly moving and is no longer even under the Antarctic continent. It lies about 200 miles north west of Cape Denison. The nearer a compass is to its attractive force, the more it exerts a downward pull on the needle or card. Marine compass cards are usually counterbalanced to allow for this force, depending on whether they are operating in the northern or southern hemisphere. But there is a practical limit, and for us the compass card had become progressively more sluggish as we sailed below 50 South. Now it was tilted down so steeply that it was effectively useless.

Ships generally use a gyro compass, which uses a high speed spinning flywheel to point to true north, irrespective of magnetic fields. But because the rate of spin needs to match the earth's rotational speed at their latitude, they are useless in polar latitudes above 75 degrees. The flywheel falls over at slow speeds. Anyway they are big, power-hungry and expensive.

Steering by our standard GPS compass display was a problem because the displayed course is affected by a time lag. The course we were looking at was actually the course we were steering a moment earlier. So we were constantly over-correcting.

Our best solution would have been one of the newly developed GPS-compasses which use multiple antennae and a tiny solid-state rate-gyro. The antennae effectively compare notes and determine where they are in relation to each other. Nice, but too expensive for a shoestring budget like ours. Even more expensive than the radar Ben had lusted after.

0145 HRS

A light breeze at last. Pity it's a head-wind though. I've reset the genoa and got her motorsailing, well off the rhumb line but at least we're moving at four knots. I've been hand-steering using the wind on my cheek and the luff of the mains'l to try to stay close-hauled. The GPS has been showing a wobbly course.

As an experiment I try hooking Sooty up to the tiller. Usually when we're motoring this doesn't work because we create our own breeze from ahead no matter which way we're going. But tonight there's just enough southerly to work the windvane and we're off on a straight GPS track. Good old Sooty.

1600 HRS

It's snowing. And it's still southerly. At least there's only about 10 knots of breeze so we can motorsail not too far off course under close-hauled main at five knots. For a while this morning we had about 20 knots and were sailing, unfortunately a long way off the rhumb. Anyway our noon run was 101 miles despite my wobbly stuff at midnight, so we're happy enough. Except for the cold of course. It's bitter and we're into multiple clothing layers all the time now. Running the engine has helped warm the cabin a bit, but Ben's concerned about our diesel consumption. We have to keep plenty in hand for the pack ice and later.

As much as possible we're doing watches perched on the companionway steps inside, with our heads in the hatch dome. The problem with that now is the snow. It's been settling on the dome and I can't see ahead. No wipers unfortunately, only my gloved hands and I have to keep going outside to clear my view.

It's 61 South and still no icebergs.

15 JANUARY
0100 HRS

It's still quite light, no real darkness at these latitudes. Ben will be happy when he comes on watch I guess. Firstly it looks like he'll win the bet. We're past 61 degrees 40 now so his guess will beat mine. Secondly we're sailing hard, driving to windward on starboard tack under triple reefed main and well rolled genoa in 25 to 30 knots of sou'westerly. And of course, thirdly, the engine has been well and truly shut down.

Ben's given up trying to sleep in the cave. It's too cold and he finds it hard getting into all his layers of warm gear in such a constrictive space. So now we're all hot bunking in the two cabin bunks. They're like cots with the lee-cloths permanently rigged. Our sleeping bags were given an airing in the warm engine compartment today, finally drying out for the first time since the knock-down. So we can come off watch straight onto a warm bunk in our own bag with another on top. Barbara's fleecy liners are great and I'm going to get a hot water bottle when I come off tonight.

By now in the voyage we were probably at the most introverted phase. We were coexisting in a semi-robotic state of mind. The routine of watch-keeping had completely taken over our lives. When not on watch, we would largely be in our bunks either sleeping or reading. It was not a morale issue. We enjoyed each others' company intensely on the occasions we were together, especially between happy hour and sched time. But the voyage had become somewhat like a visit to the dentist, stretched into several days. Psychologically we had to close our eyes and put up with the discomfort in the knowledge that it would eventually be over. That's where the books came in. They were like our anaesthetic.

Snow Petrel had a big library. A whole box full of books in the back of the starboard fo'cs'le locker. We'd each chosen an assortment before we left, and were now devouring them voraciously. I liked a tossed salad approach – a good light adventure followed by a non-fiction (probably something Antarctic in content) followed perhaps by something humorous. Matt sauced his entire day with music – we seldom saw him without headphones whether reading or sleeping. His flavours in books were more inclined towards fantasy series, while Ben was most partial to a curious mismatch of science fiction and nautical non-fiction. But we essentially were all omnivorous, and would often snatch each others' discards for a taste of something new.

2100 HRS

It's getting tedious. We've been hard on the wind all day. It's been varying between 15 and 25 knots, between sou'easterly and sou'westerly, so we've been tacking for the best VMG. Matt had a hard job cooking a stew tonight. Harder than last night's pizza. But he's happy. He's won the iceberg bet by default. We're just coming up to 63 South now and STILL no icebergs. The little rat! He wanted his beer at dinner but Ben and I won't let him till we actually see one.

On tonight's sched Mike tells us that these southerlies could last two more days. But the good news is that the latest colour-coded NOAA ice charts show only green between us and land. That's only one-tenth pack ice. If it's true, then we should have an easy run through it. But our VMG is only averaging two and a half knots so, unless things improve, it'll take another four days to cover the last 250 miles even if the pack doesn't slow us.

So frustrating.

16 JANUARY
0600 HRS

Matt's grumbling about our slow progress as I take over from him, and as I scan the horizon I spot not one but *two* icebergs. Gleefully I break the news to him as he crawls into the bunk I've just vacated. He takes my gloating in good humour and reminds me that he will drink his beer in front of us both later. Meanwhile Ben stirs himself long enough to poke his head up into the dome for a quick look, clad in his thermal underwear, before diving back into his bunk for another two hours' sleep.

There's something magical about our first two icebergs. We pass one during Ben's watch, an interestingly sculpted castle of a berg with a turret at each end. Down to leeward is the other berg, a tabular one probably a mile long but relatively boring in its rectangularity. Matt wants us to sail close to it but Ben doesn't want to waste too much time, so we pose for some shots before Matt and I crawl back into our bunks for more sleep.

These two icebergs were probably spawned in different locations, but both would have been drifting slowly towards the west at over half a knot in the circumpolar current. The tabular berg would possibly have calved off a shelf in the Ross Sea in recent years and been carried out by the current. Or perhaps it may have broken away from the Mertz glacier, then grounded a while before drifting out to sea at the mercy of wind and current.

Our first iceberg—a castle—earned me a watch in bed

For someone who just lost a bet, Ben was happy to have achieved his second goal

The castle berg would have been at sea for much longer, drifting at the mercy of the erosive forces of sun, wind and waves. It may have even capsized at some point in its history, in which case we would have been looking at its eroded roots.

1200 HRS

I feel rather guilty lying here in my bunk when I should be going on watch. It's a bit like taking a sicky from work when you don't really deserve one. After all, it was mostly my good luck that those bergs happened along during my watch.

But Matt tells me not to be stupid, says that if only he'd looked around better this morning he'd have been the lucky one – we wouldn't have been able to drag him out for his watch. Ben agrees. So I settle back in my bunk cheerfully and toast them both with a double nip of neat rum from the bottle provided for celebratory purposes by our great friends Nick and Taff Gales. I'm reading 'The Restaurant at the End of the Universe' and somehow it seems appropriate.

Matt's frying up pikelets for an iceberg day celebration and from my bunk, I film my sons enjoying themselves. We're a team and have come alive again.

The two of them have split the afternoon into two three hour watches, and we're tacking into 15 knots of southerly – frustratingly slow but not too demanding for them, unless you count the occasional foray out to wipe snow off the dome. The noon run was only 71 miles but there's not far to go. There's an air of expectancy now.

17 JANUARY
0600 HRS

At last another iceberg. Twenty-four hours since the first ones. We expected there'd be dozens by now. This one's shaped like a cathedral with a spire. Ben's happy this morning, a change from being grumpy last night when we had to motor for six hours in a very light head wind. His 2200 hr log entry simply read 'bloody motor' which sums up his attitude to yacht engines. It pains him to be dependent on one for a trip like this.

This cathedral is not far out of our way, and Matt's sneaked us quite close to it during his watch so he can photograph it. It's definitely an old capsized berg and we shoot far more film than we need to, before Ben vetos Matt's plan to sail right around it. Ben's spooked about its brash field. Satisfied enough, we push on and I wriggle down aft to top up the gearbox oil, a job which requires removing a few panels from the radio-cave wall. Unfortunately the wind chooses this time to freshen up to 20 knots again so it's both smelly and joggly down there, but my stomach is immune to those horrors now. When I finally come up for air there's quite a lot of white in the water, a mixture of whitecaps and bergy bits. We won't be doing any reading on watch any more.

There are now eight bergs visible around us, mostly big tabular ones. No-one's said anything about the need for increased vigilance but generally there are two of us up at a time now. Perhaps that's why Ben and I notice a pod of whales not far off to starboard. They're travelling at an angle to our track so we don't see any tails, only their puffs of steam like little grey clouds. Meanwhile I see a pure white albatross and spend half an hour hunting through the book until I realise that it must be a rare form of giant petrel.

Each iceberg is constantly shedding chunks of ice. Occasionally we saw one actually break away and dive deep into the surrounding water. The spectacular bit was yet to come when it would re-emerge high in the air like a whale breaching.

These chunks gradually drift away to leeward as a random series of large and small pieces like a floating reef about two or three miles long. It is known as a brash field, and most bergs have one. To us newcomers it seemed frighteningly sinister, and we would tack to windward of many large bergs rather than thread our way through their brash.

2000 HRS

I'm in the engine compartment again. Ben's concerned about the gearbox, a concern he's had since we left and which has heightened now that we're close to so many dangers. It's an old Chinese double-clutch hydraulic-shift model which is dependent on having good oil pressure. But the pressure gauge has been jumping around every time we've checked it and Ben doesn't like the way it rattles.

I'm a lot more relaxed about it, but this isn't my boat. And I must admit it's not in my nature to worry until things stop working. Certainly this gearbox has been losing oil every time we run it for a few hours so this time I'm going over it with a fine toothcomb. The southerly has eased to ten knots and the sea has flattened out so it's a good time to check the level while we're not bouncing around or heeling. Outside there are bergy bits scattered all over the place but we've shut the engine down in a good clear patch of water.

I'm not really worried about the gearbox falling apart. We've got a similar British model on *New Zealand Maid* and I know there's a manual over-ride. Ben points out that it takes time to engage the over-ride, and that it only gives us forward gear, not reverse. The Tasmanian marine engineer we talked to before we left didn't seem too worried about the odd rattle in it. He assured us that it should be nearly bulletproof, then gave us a few hints on how to strip it down and patch it up if necessary.

But Ben's right that we need to maintain the correct oil level. If we end up somewhere inside the pack, we won't need the stress of regular engine shut-downs. So now we're trying a few ways to ferret out this elusive leak.

Eureka! I spot the problem. I could see it as soon as Ben started it up for me just then. It only dribbles out when the engine's running so it hasn't been much of an issue on our sail south. And it's easy to plug – just a missing bolt from a plate on top. I have it fixed in a minute or two. At least I've earned my stripes as ship's engineer as well as cabin-boy. And Ben looks a lot happier.

We're ready for the pack.

Our first view of the pack on the southern horizon

PHASE 4

The Pack Ice

I strayed inside a minefield once. A minefield of rocks it was – an utterly terrifying place to be under sail. On the chart it showed up as a shaded blue semicircle, randomly studded with crosses, curving nearly three miles out from the lower east coast of New Zealand's North Island to a single outlying visible rock.

I'd turned in at 0400 hrs, trusting the helm to the dawn watch and giving a course which would maintain a five mile offing. The helmsman was a relation of the owner for this delivery. Compass steering is an acquired skill and competence should be proven, not assumed, especially in those pre-GPS days. My mistake!

I was torn from the deep sleep of a broken watch by the sound of an idling outboard alongside and an unsympathetic voice: 'Hey mate, you're inside the black stump!' I'll swear I grew my first grey hair that dawn, as we gingerly retraced our wake, a lookout posted aloft.

I have relived the horror of that incident in my sleep on many occasions since, the kind of nightmare in which one flounders helplessly amidst a thousand unseen dangers.

17 JANUARY
2230 HRS

On the horizon ahead I see a low wall of white and gold. To the south-west the sun hangs poised on the horizon emitting a golden light which reflects off the bergs around us. To the north-east a nearly full moon glows in a pale blue

The midnight view to the north, following a lead inside the pack

sky. We've reshuffled the watches today so I've got the evening watch. Ben is asleep and I delay calling him up until I'm sure the white horizon is not a mere trick of light. Twenty minutes later there's no doubt left. We're motoring on a flat calm sea towards a seemingly impenetrable barrier, a jumble of white and golden shapes, angular and random quite unlike the flat rafts of pancake ice I had envisaged.

Ben emerges from his bunk, suddenly awake and focused. This is a moment we have been expecting for some hours, and he scans the approaching ice edge with binoculars, searching for an opening to lead us in. Hearing our excited talk Matt surfaces too, camera in hand – as always – and stifling a yawn. The photographer in him registers the colours, the sheer beauty of this setting, an artist's delight as he considers shutter speeds and lens selection.

I marvel at how two people can focus on such different aspects when placed in an identical situation: Ben, the navigator/skipper, ever the practical one, and Matt, the artist, both from the same gene pool, yet such unique and distinct individuals.

The visible horizon from *Snow Petrel*'s cockpit, height of eye two metres, is only about three miles, and at five knots it doesn't take long to close the pack edge. There is barely time to boil a kettle and break out some celebratory chocolate. Ben has donned gloves, dork hat and harness already and is preparing to run up the ratlines to the spreaders where he can scan ahead for leads. It's going to be a long and memorable night, even if it is one of perpetual light. We have reached 65 degrees 43 minutes South and are seventy-seven miles from the ice cliffs of Antarctica.

As the sun's lower limb angles ever so slowly to dip below the south-western horizon we reach the ice. With no radiant warmth, the air has a bite which numbs the lips and we find ourselves struggling to talk coherently. From aloft, Ben has identified a passage in, and standing with the tiller between my legs I steer us into this uncharted minefield.

Don MacIntyre had briefed us at some length on the pack ice experience. As a mentor he was invaluable. He spoke of its extreme beauty and its extreme danger. He was accurate on both counts.

'Whatever you do,' he had warned, 'never enter the pack without seeing where the lead will take you. And always watch behind to check your entry lead stays open.'

Ben had done plenty of homework about the ice too. He had downloaded many summers' worth of ice-charts for the area from the Ross Sea to west of Dumont D'Urville Base. They were an interesting series of maps, colour-coded to show patterns of ice density in tenths of cover. Anything over three-tenths would be effectively impenetrable to a vessel of Snow Petrel's *size with her mere 3 mm of steel plating. The nice green patches of one-tenth were what we liked to see.*

It was the past decade's trends that Ben had been looking for, to determine when would be the earliest likelihood of making it through to the coast, and when would be the latest we could expect to safely extricate ourselves. His conclusion was a six week window from the end of December to mid February.

Two other interesting conclusions could be drawn from the exercise. Firstly there was almost always an inland sea, free of ice, just off the coast near Cape Denison. This, we learned, was a product of the extreme katabatic winds simply blowing any ice out to sea as it forms. Secondly the tongue of ice which sweeps out of the Ross Sea and westward past Cape Denison toward the French territory becomes progressively thinner as it travels west. The conclusion: if in doubt go west – eventually there should be a way through, even if it takes days.

And as we entered the pack that dusk, the question on all our minds was which way to go at the first roadblock – east or west?

2245 HRS

Our entry into this icy realm seems unexpectedly familiar. We are motoring through what feels like a typical large river mouth, about a hundred metres wide and flanked by lumpy white stopbanks. We even have a few spectators waving. Miniature tuxedo-clad figures are staring at us in bewilderment from their icy viewpoints, flapping their arms excitedly before hopping to the water's edge on their comical little legs and launching themselves clumsily into the freezing waters.

From his perch far above me, Ben is scanning the distant expanse of white. With the engine running I struggle to hear what he has to say. Matt is in movie-maker's heaven, surveying the scene from his viewfinder and fussing about battery life in these temperatures. He alternates between the camcorder and his stills camera. I marvel that they both have survived the abuse of salt spray and ungentle handling during the voyage down.

Our warm drinks are ideal for thawing frozen fingers. Steering as I am with the tiller between my thighs, I can cradle my mug between both hands and absorb the heat. Aloft, Ben has no such luxury and has resorted to a chemical equivalent. The little gel heat packs we purchased a lifetime ago in Hobart, magically burst into glorious heat with the flick of an embedded metal disc. Space age technology at its best.

Ben is gesticulating excitedly at something and I follow his gaze. A pair of white winged shapes is sweeping effortlessly astern of us, much more swiftly than the albatrosses and petrels we have become used to over the southern ocean rollers. Their agility and energy is breathtaking and briefly they slide across the face of the moon.

'Snow petrels,' shouts Ben, although both Matt and I have already identified these beautiful creatures. Matt's doing his best to capture them on film but they're far too elusive for his long lens to track.

Meanwhile we're fast approaching a solid line of east-west ice. Ben signals for me to turn to port but remembering the 'go west' axiom I forget my lowly place as cabin-boy, and query his call. From down here at deck level the starboard lead looks pretty clear too. Mistake! It's the first time Ben has seriously pulled rank on me and he leaves no doubt who's captain of this ship. He doesn't actually say much, but it is his air of authority, earned during years of responsibility on big ship bridge-decks, that puts me firmly in my place. Chastened and mindful of my promises, I turn to port.

Seven years earlier a sixty foot aluminium sloop ventured into these waters on a charter passage in the hope of landing at Cape Denison. It made it

*through the thinning January ice to be thwarted only a few miles off Cape
Denison by the notorious katabatic gales which stopped it dead in its tracks.
After two days' attempts to claw their way into the haven of Boat Harbour,
the disheartened crew turned northward towards Hobart – straight into the
hungry jaws of the pack.*

*After allowing them safe passage southwards, the ice minefield was not
going to let them off so lightly this time. As they reached the midst of the pack
they watched in horror as both their exit and entry leads slammed shut. The
grinding floes closed in on their victim and the crew found themselves locked
in a surging heaving mass of ice – thousands of tonnes battering the hull into
a panel-beaten lump of alloy.*

Memories of the crushing and sinking of Shackleton's Endurance, *and
more recently the ice-strengthened* Southern Quest *in the nearby Ross Sea,
must have haunted the crew as the days passed – jostled and squeezed by
countless tonnes of floes.*

*Their fate was a happier one than they may have expected, with a
reprieve eventually opening an exit lead and allowing them to limp northwards,
ever wondering whether the unpredictable Southern Ocean would allow their
vulnerable hull to return to her home port.*

18 JANUARY
0100 HRS

For over two hours we've been tracking eastward through an ice channel
which stretches as far as the eye can see to the east. Embedded in the pack
are several distinctive large icebergs which give the surreal terrain a false
sense of permanence. Like isolated hills arising from a blue-white plain
these bergs are useful as steering references as we motor slowly along this
wide lead. It is not a totally open channel, but the small isolated bergy bits
scattered across our path are easy to avoid and pose no threat as long as we
retain our guard.

Ben is back in the cockpit now and I take the opportunity to climb the
spreaders and survey the pack to our south. It is completely different from my
earlier expectations. Rather than a solid mass of flat ice, this pack is a mixture
of old and new sea ice, many shapes betraying a lengthy period afloat, as
the upturned roots of decaying bergy bits wallow drunkenly among angular
corners of newer ice.

What particularly strikes me is the banded nature of this phenomenon.
It is as if Antarctica, like Saturn, is surrounded by rings. The belt beside

My view from below …   … and Ben's from aloft

us is just one of a number of similar east-west belts cutting us off from our destination. To find an opening through the first wall would allow us only fifty or so metres to the next, and so on for as far as the limited southern horizon would reveal.

The southern sky is a radiant pink, lit by a sun which is tracking eastwards barely out of sight below the horizon. Dusk and dawn have fused into a single transitional light-filled phase, and only one star is visible, more likely a planet, glowing in a pale blue sky.

Back on deck, I can see that Ben is worried. A light northerly has picked up and the whole field is beginning to move. At this stage, everything is moving in synch, and our channel is not squeezing up, but we wonder about the status of our entry lead a dozen or more miles astern. Ever mindful of Don MacIntyre's warnings, Ben calls our eastward search off and we begin to backtrack, noting how much our inbound GPS track has already been displaced sidewards.

Ben's knowledge of the nature of our surroundings is unexpected for someone who is as new to it as I am. For him, this experience is the culmination of years of reading and personal interest. He points out the differences between multi-year ice and sea ice, between heavy pack and three-tenths. But his face is a picture of exultation mixed with concern. The burden of responsibility is sitting more heavily on his shoulders than ever before in this adventure, and it has become clear to all three of us that he is the ice-master in comparison to Matt's and my comparative naivety.

Someone needs to go below for an off-watch. Reluctantly I volunteer. This is the experience of a lifetime and I'm lapping it up, but we are going to have to discipline ourselves over the coming hours to husband our sleep despite the temptation to stay on deck. The consequences of fatigue are too dire, and it is now that the value of having three rather than two to share helming duties is most apparent.

Six weeks before our departure Ben hauled Snow Petrel *out on the Kettering slipway. It was a family sort of occasion as Barbara and I had* New Zealand Maid *in the cradle next door for a few important maintenance jobs. We even rigged an awning between the two boats as a rain shelter. Ben was hard at work welding up almost all his through-hull openings and fitting ice-guards to protrusions such as his depth-sounder transducer. His worst moment was the realisation that his propeller shaft and its coupling was beyond repair and needed some expensive engineering. This was his darkest hour and nearly spelt the end of his plans before we were fully committed to help him.*

It was the conversations we had during this week of high activity that awoke me to some of the special considerations involved in planning a trip to such icy temperatures. Some people even switch propellors from bronze to cast iron. At zero degrees, bronze can become so brittle that it might shatter like glass if it hits a chunk of ice.

Another issue was the freezing of water-tanks. Snow Petrel*'s tanks, like those in most steel boats, utilise the hull plating as an outside wall. Seawater freezes at more than a degree below zero, and as a result our water-tanks would become like a typical chest freezer, turning our fresh water into a tank-shaped block of ice.*

Similarly diesel undergoes its own transformation at low temperatures, potentially waxing out at sub-zero temperatures. In Tasmania the diesel sold at the bowsers is different in summer from winter, and it became another challenge – only days before Christmas – for Ben to locate and purchase sufficient winter-grade additive to render his existing diesel safe for the Antarctic conditions.

0400 HRS

I awake from a deep sleep to the sensation of an abrupt change in engine revs. Matt is climbing down the companionway ladder and I know my cosy time is done. I signal to him, and he returns to the helm while I boil the kettle and pull on layers of clothing. The GPS shows our track as 170 True – nearly due south – and puzzled, I carry my cuppa into the cockpit for an explanation. Outside the sun is well established in the south-eastern sky, and Matt explains that once they had motored out through our initial entry lead, Ben had gone below leaving him to follow the ice-edge westward until another clear lead opened up. He had found himself curving more to the south into a wide opening like a big bay, and was now ready to hand over and let me ascertain whether it was a blind bay or a break between two huge separate masses of pack.

Alone in the cockpit with the engine ticking over at low revs, I enjoy the unimaginable colours of the ice-scape around me. I've heard that the Inuit people have a multitude of names for ice and snow as well as the colour we know as 'white'. Now I can see why. Some of the decaying bergy bits glow turquoise and emerald, and others are layered in browns and yellows, occasionally horizontal, but usually at various angles betraying repeated capsizes during the process of decay.

After two hours moving steadily southwards it becomes clear *Snow Petrel* is running out of clear water. It's not that this wide lead is narrowing but rather that it's becoming too choked with random chunks of loose pack for us to continue safely. In Ben's terms, I guess we are motoring into four-tenths pack, and I simply can't manoeuvre around one without risking collision with the next. My real fear is the submerged shelves which lurk around the edges of the larger heavily decayed bergs. Sure, they show up as a green patch of water, but only from close quarters.

I take her out of gear and wait for us to lose way. Ben, not surprisingly, shows up almost immediately, looking rather the worse for wear. He takes in the situation immediately and waits for me to run aloft. He doesn't seem surprised with my disappointing conclusion that there's no open sea in sight for as far as my lofty eye can see. There is no other option than to backtrack once more, this time to the north, and he disappears below again to grab a little more sleep while the going is safe.

The pack ice in this part of the world is the product of a multitude of phenomena. Three months earlier the sea here would have been solid ten-tenths, and the poor emperor penguins would have been trudging across it en route to their feathered spouses and fluffy offspring. The flatter thinner slabs are the sea ice, survivors from the previous winter, weakened by the radiant heat of a twenty two hour sun and broken away from a vast plain of metre-thick ice by the ocean swells. The crazy angular stuff is probably multi-year sea ice, slabs which have been jammed together and fused during successive winters while joining forces with the new season's frozen surface.

The larger chunks are likely to be fragments of ancient icebergs, calved off the cliff-like walls and sculpted by waves, wind and sun. Many are inverted or on their sides, their original orientation indicated by striations which owe their origins to horizontal layers of precipitation and dust or moraine particles at some location far inland. Perhaps even Pompei and Vesuvius are represented in this visual feast.

The babies of the pack are the bits of brash, particles ranging in size from pots and pans to kitchen tables. Even these pose a risk for Snow Petrel *at any speed. We had to keep reminding ourselves that only ten percent of anything floating here was visible. The invisible ninety percent lurking beneath the surface contained a mass and water-resistance akin to a sizable chunk of rock.*

0730 HRS

I've been motoring nor-nor'west for an hour now, and have managed to feed myself some cereal in the process. But there now appears to be an open lead to the west, and once again I call Ben up. It's Ben's boat and Ben's voyage. After decades of sailing as skipper myself, I know how important it is to acknowledge his ultimate responsibility. Especially in my junior position as his father.

This time he joins me in full gear, and understandably opts for the western lead. At least now we aren't motoring away from Antarctica. An hour later there is the distinct feel of movement, the heaving restlessness of an ocean swell accompanied by the rumbling and grinding of ice moving around us. With it is the growing sensation of wind, and with little other warning we re-emerge into an open sea of whitecaps generated by a stiff westerly breeze.

It's strange to be pitching and heeling again after the deceptive calmness of the pack. Ben soon has us sailing under double reefed main and full heads'l, rather to my concern. I can see where he's coming from; after all, diesel must be conserved wherever possible, but to me this is potentially the most dangerous phase of our trip yet. I stand in the biting cold wind next to the windward shrouds, searching the water ahead for growlers and brash. There's plenty around us, disguised as innocent whitecaps as we pitch and heel on a reach to the south. Dropping off a wave now at six knots onto a big chunk of ice would make a lot worse mess in this seaway than bumping into one last night at four knots in the calm.

Matt emerges, pink and refreshed, curious at our motion. His expression turns to alarm at seeing Ben helming hard to avoid large chunks of ice, as we plunge through lively seas. Matt has shown up at a particularly spectacular moment. To windward is a large berg and we're sailing through its brash field.

With all three of us now on deck we can share the lookout and helming duties, and the tension eases. We're getting used to sharing our waves with these obstacles, and we take turns to grab a substantial lunch while enjoying each other's company.

Back in the third gear phase of our preparations we had discussed at length the risks of collision with a growler. Ben had already given the matter a lot of thought and concluded that a direct hit on the stem would not necessarily spell disaster. The heavy steel flat-bar would absorb much of the impact as the bow rode up and the boat slowed. Our biggest danger would be a glancing blow, Titanic *style, with a large chunk sliding past one side of the hull to tear a gash through the 3 mm steel like a giant can-opener.*

So Ben set Matt to work sealing up a collision semi-bulkhead under the forward bunk to add to the buoyancy already afforded by the smaller anchor-locker bulkhead. Any puncture aft of this would need to be fothered – wrapped with a sail or tarp from outside or sealed from inside with something jammed against it.

To Ben's four-man liferaft we had added New Zealand Maid*'s six-man one. Then Don and Margie MacIntyre had added two survival suits to Ben's existing one. It should have been very comforting. However we were very aware that it would be an extremely long time to be floating around in icy waters before anyone might show, down there among the pack. Hopefully the 406 EPIRB, our emergency button to the satellites, might raise an ear somewhere in the ether. Better still, don't hit anything.*

1230 HRS

Once again we've reached the pack, but at least we've made good ten more miles towards Antarctica. The breeze has eased to about ten knots and the ice has killed the seas. It's as if we've entered a maze now and the pack has a different feel from last night. Gone are Saturn's rings. In their place is a confusing labyrinth of leads. We're still under sail, and surprisingly I'm enjoying the challenge. At our mere three or four knots of boat speed, and without the seaway, the danger seems diminished. Ben is spending a lot of time aloft and has a strong hunch that there is open water not too far to the

A fresh lead appears to our port

Approaching five-tenths pack

south. From his vantage point, he's cheating the maze and directs me left and right into ever-narrowing fresh leads. Matt is filming furiously, both on deck and up in the spreaders.

I'm finding it a strain to continue under sail. Ben directs me into a tiny four metre wide gulch and I let go all sheets to reduce our way. As we ghost through the gap, I watch the pale green of a shallow shelf directly beneath our starboard side. My inability to control our speed is becoming a strain. Thankfully Ben doesn't need prompting. Sails are doused and the intrusive noise of our engine spoils the solitude. No-one complains.

According to Ben's judgement we are now negotiating five-tenths ice surrounded with nine-tenths pack. Its saving grace is its layout. And the fact that there is unmistakably open sea only two hundred metres to our south. The

Free of the pack. Ben's next goal   … and Matt is an equally happy chappy
achieved …

A kite run through an inland sea—next stop Antarctica

ice here is big multi-year stuff. At deck level we can't see over it. It's truly a maze and without our mast to view it from, we'd be in trouble. Ben's strategy is to zigzag our way through the tiny leads, and if necessary nudge up to an obstacle and use the engine to shove it laboriously out of our way. Thankfully we don't need that option.

At five o'clock in the afternoon we emerge from the pack. It's an abrupt exit from a high wall of ice to blue open sea, with barely a speck of brash in sight ahead. We are at 66 degrees 30 minutes South. Antarctica is a mere thirty miles away across open waters. But where? At this distance, the coast should be visible. We scan the horizon in perplexity but below the distant line of light grey cloud is nothing but a horizon of blue sea.

Then the revelation hits me. It's so obvious that I can't believe how easily our eyes have deceived us. Ben and Matt are at work raising full main and spinnaker. I shout to them in glee. Cloud line – phooee! That's the grey-white skyline of the great continent itself. It's probably been visible all day.

ANTARCTICA, HERE WE COME!

The grey cloud reveals itself

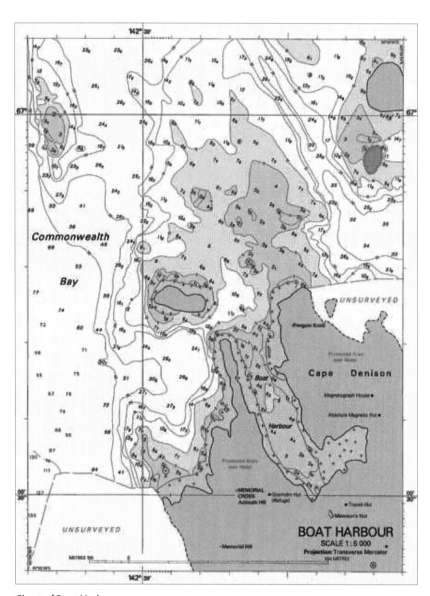

Chart of Boat Harbour

PHASE 5

Cape Denison at Last

The Cape Denison katabatic winds are notorious. The immediate area is known as the windiest place on the planet. Statistically there is no other sea-level location which experiences such a proportion of its year battered by intense winds. Maybe somewhere atop the Himalayas is an equal, but the air is a lot less dense up there. To the best of my knowledge no weather station has matched its intensity.

According to our Antarctic Pilot data there are 284 days of gales or stronger each year. Mawson regularly recorded gusts approaching 200 knots during his two years of records. The only months of significant reprieve are December and January. So our chances of being hammered were reduced to one day in two.

Don MacIntyre had warned us we may well arrive to a katabatic gale. If so it would be pointless trying to punch our way in. They lose their strength a few miles offshore, he had advised us. Better to shelter behind a grounded berg and wait for it to ease.

DAY ONE: 19 JANUARY
0100 HRS

This is a landfall like I've never experienced before. It's not the shape so much as the lack of colour. The approaching cliffs look very much like typical coastal cliffs, except that these ones are albino. Their whiteness is broken only by occasional smudges of grey, very different from the yellows and browns I'm used to. And the cliff-tops, which I'm programmed to expect as green, are simply more of the same whiteness merging into a featureless smear of grey where the skyline meets the sky, devoid of any mountain range or even a single angle.

But we've been lucky with the wind. True there's been a 25 knot southerly for much of the evening, and we hove-to behind a large iceberg for a while to get the big anchor on deck and inflate the tinker, but now as the GPS counts us down the last few miles, we're motoring easily in a moderate offshore breeze.

The sun has been skulking behind the skyline – or the dome as Ben calls it – for a couple of hours, but it's still daylight. We're just inside the Antarctic circle now and (drat) we missed a celebration. Never mind, there'll be a big one soon enough. But I'm chilled to the bone. There's a relentless bite to that breeze which cuts like a knife, especially now there's no solar warmth.

Matt yells something and points. His eyes must be sharper than we thought. There on the grey-black promontory ahead is a cross, silhouetted starkly against the rose-tinted sky. We've read about the tragedy of Mawson's expedition, and the huge cross that he had erected to ease the pain of Ninnis' and Mertz's deaths. And there it stands, over ninety years later, a poignant reminder of the historic interface between nature's impartiality and human endurance.

An Australian geologist, Douglas Mawson (later Sir) handpicked a team of professional and amateur scientists to establish three bases in Antarctica in 1912. Arriving later than planned, his team built a significant hut here, thrilled to have stumbled upon an ice-free promontory with a sheltered little boat harbour. It was the only mainland hut his team built, although a smaller group continued along the coast to settle for a season on an iceshelf.

Mawson's group suffered terribly as the continent proceeded to unleash phenomenal quantities of sub-zero air down hundreds of miles of its slopes directly into their valley. 'Home of the Blizzard' he called it, and the name has stuck.

What Mawson hadn't known was the broader topography of this region. Behind his hut for hundreds of miles is a natural channel which funnels the already accelerating downflow of cold katabatic air from the inland icecap, thousands of metres high, into this stretch of coastline. It wasn't too obvious for Mawson's team in January. The high pressure systems just offshore were often holding it at bay like a big dam. But as the Lows started tracking past, like giant vacuum cleaners, the pent-up cold air mass was being sucked past their hut at unbelievable velocities.

And now we were poking our nose into this little meteorological lottery.

0130 HRS

With the chartlet on hand, and Don MacIntyre's advice firmly in mind, we motor under Cape Denison, turn right at the one-third point across the entrance to Boat Harbour, and creep slowly into the inlet towards Mawson's Hut. The sounder rises to less than three metres as we watch, then levels off.

Even above the clatter of *Snow Petrel*'s diesel we can hear an awful din, an unfamiliar staccato braying noise filling the air from every direction. But we are too preoccupied to fully register the sheer numbers of Adélie penguins clustered among the grey and white landscape we have entered.

I'm on the foredeck struggling with the lashings on the giant fisherman anchor loaned to us by our mate Donough a few days before departure. It's been on deck for only an hour but is already caked with frozen seaspray. Matt is somewhere behind me filming continuously. My gloved fingers refuse to work. The delicate operation of untying even a simple slipknot is beyond my power. In desperation I resort to a knife as Ben repeats his call more urgently to let go anchor. *Snow Petrel*'s bow is beginning to sheer away towards the eastern rocks as the chain rattles out. Twenty, thirty, forty metres. I throw a couple of turns on the bollard to let her pull up, then turn to Ben for his intentions. Too much chain and we could sheer from side to side, crunching rocks in the process. 'Let go the lot!' His command is so decisive I don't even query it. Sixty metres is a lot of chain and a lot of caternary holding power. We may need every metre of it in here.

0330 HRS

Ben and Matt are still at work. I'm glad it's them not me out there. The tinker looked like a toffee apple when we launched it, glazed in a smooth layer of ice. And the outboard took ages to start, despite Ben's precaution of checking it was working earlier, back in the shelter of that iceberg.

I've got the easy job. They both wanted to set foot on land straight away which was fine by me. It's like a freezer out there and I'm happy to wait till later when the sun's well up.

So my function is to keep the kettle and thermos full of hot water, and to feed rope to Ben and Matt out of this giant coil as they search the shore for suitable fastening points. The advantage of being in charge of hot water is that I get to mind the hotwater bottles while the boys are playing around ashore. I've found some good spots to mind them too. Two stuffed inside my jacket and another wrapped in a towel where I can put my hands in very regularly to check it's still warm.

Snow Petrel lies snug in Cape Denison's Boat Harbour at last. And in such weather …

Something's happened. I watch them drop a line and come flying back. Matt looks terrified. Ben explains that they think a leopard seal was about to attack them. I lend them the hotties and feed them hot drinks and chocolate while we hunt through the books for pictures of seal breeds. There's one that looks exactly right, dark brown covered with elongated spots. It's only a harmless little Weddell seal, wanting to play with the boys and their nice rope. Abashed, they retrieve the floating loose end and go back to their task.

Shore-lines are a great way to snug a boat into a tight anchorage. We've done it for years. The risk comes when the boat is side-on to a gale with a stern-line acting against a bow anchor. The vectors involved add an enormous load to both lines. Usually it's the anchor that drags, unless the tree-branch snaps on the shore-line. I've experienced both failures over the years, and Barbara now hates any stern-line. A pity, because they can be safe and very useful.

In Boat Harbour at Cape Denison, the wind directions should be very predictable. Katabatics should come from the south, directly ahead. Other gales associated with Lows could come from the east or southeast. Nothing very significant should come from north or west. So we were snugging Snow Petrel *into a cat's cradle of shore-lines, secured to wire-rope strops around big boulders, or in one case, to a spare anchor embedded in a cleft ashore.*

Two went at an angle from either side of the bow, and two more angled ashore from the stern quarter cleats. The fifth was a breastline from a central cleat, at right angles to the eastern shore. The big anchor became almost obsolete, which wasn't a bad thing as we couldn't fully rely on the bottom holding power. There could be seaweed, gravel or a smooth rock surface down there. And we wanted to stay put if a hundred knot gale happened along.

0530 HRS

Secure at last. The boys are done. But we're all buzzing, a babble of talk. We've actually done it. Made it to Antarctica. It somehow doesn't seem real.

We're all sitting on the settees, lee cloths hanging for the first time since Tasmania. A rich hot chocolate for everyone and a hot-water bottle each while we talk. The sun's already well up, but time has become irrelevant.

I break out the rum. There are no watches to keep now. And we talk. Talk. Talk. It all pours out, two months' worth of hopes and fears, of aspirations and trepidations, all compressed into ninety minutes' worth of words.

None of us has ever dared express total confidence that we would achieve this landfall. So much could have gone wrong. Even getting *Snow Petrel* into a fit state for departure was in question until the last minute. And then there was so much that could have gone wrong. Storms, dismasting, ice-collisions, engine or transmission failure, injury…. Yet here we are, our little team, unscathed and in good spirits.

The rum loosens our tongues and the banter begins. I pour a second glass all round then squirrel the bottle away for another occasion. No point exploring tomorrow with sore heads. We talk of best and worst moments, remember past voyages, talk of practicalities. We are a team, a bunch of good mates.

Then sleep, glorious glorious sleep.

To venture ashore onto the Antarctic continent requires a permit. Ours could only be issued by the country of citizenship of the master. We are all New Zealanders by birth, but Ben was aware of potential difficulties gaining a permit from Kiwi authorities for a non-scientific excursion without a variety of complex hurdles.

The Australian authorities appeared to have a more comfortable attitude towards trips like ours. And with the Australian Antarctic Division situated only a few kilometres from our marina, it seemed logical that Ben should apply for an environmental permit there. As a dual citizen he had this choice.

His application went through without a hitch, and all had seemed well until shortly before Christmas when he was informed that his permit was revoked until he could prove adequate insurance. But what type of insurance? No-one at the Division could really say. And it was obvious to all that no self-respecting company would be issuing insurance of any type, so close to Christmas, for a venture like this. Fortunately, reason prevailed over bureaucracy – they are decent people in there at the Division – so he came back from his meeting smiling and waving a sheaf of papers. Once all three of us had signed a set of promises and indemnities we were free to go.

1330 HRS

Sleep – heavy and uninterrupted. No alarms. No watch calls. Sleep until one of us musters the will to get up. Me of course, as always – the call of the bladder and curiosity, an awakening eagerness. Time for a cuppa. Porridge anyone?

Ben's stirring now. He drinks his tea lying face down in the cave, cup against his cheek, dozing between mouthfuls.

Matt wallows in his big black sleeping bag, just another seal down here, unable to break through into consciousness, always the last to come alive.

There's an interminable time lapse between waking and getting ashore. In a former life I've found when organising school parties that this lead-time increases exponentially in relation to the number in the party. But why does it take only three of us so long to get organised?

The whole cabin is a cramped little burrow, full of gear. Wet clothes, ropes, jerry cans. Moving about is like a cube game. To get into the galley means that someone has to perch on the companionway steps while someone else sucks in and squeezes against the mast compression post. When we had one person continuously on watch and another in bed this wasn't an issue.

Where's my coat? – Has anyone seen my glove? – The blue one? – My hat's gone! – My socks are wet! …. At last we're ashore. It's mid afternoon, the sky is a hard blue, the sun is shining and best of all, there's no wind. So much for the Windiest Place in the World.

Ben's inflatable and outboard were not quite the stuff of modern expeditions. The tinker dinghy was twenty years old and well patched. He sent it in for a professional patch-up before we left but somehow its shabbiness caused it to be relegated to a dark corner while the staff focused on much more important servicings – liferafts for race yachts. So we patched it again ourselves.

When I went to collect the ancient two horse outboard from its service it still hadn't been done either. It had been in for three weeks already and there was only a week left till Christmas. I made the mistake of telling the mechanic what it was needed for. Luckily I didn't let on that I was part of Ben's crazy trip.

The Adélie penguins hadn't signed any pledge to keep away from us when we landed

'Tell him he's a fool! – This outboard's crap! – He'll need at least fifteen horsepower down there! – And he's a fool to even think of sailing down!'

The guy used to be an engineer on the Australian icebreaker and had done a dozen terrifying trips south. He knew best. But at least it was ready next day.

So we were warned, and had to heed the potential unreliability. It would be more than embarrassing to be blown out of Boat Harbour in a hundred knot gale. Ben – ever the mad inventor – set up a pair of harness straps to attach the tinker to a shore-line like a sliding rail. That way, even if the outboard died we could pull ourselves back to safety in a blow. And in case anyone became trapped ashore, he lashed a survival suit, emergency gear and a cheap inflatable canoe to a safe spot on the shore.

1600 HRS

The wonder of it all. As we step ashore we are greeted by the effervescent curiosity of the Adélie penguins. Nature's comics. Evolution has played a trick on these ever-so-cute little creatures, giving them such stumpy little legs and hobbit feet. Everywhere they waddle and hop is like a sack race. We have solemnly agreed not to approach the wildlife closer than fifteen metres, but

Mawson couldn't believe his luck finding a boat harbour site for his famous hut

The Baltic pine exterior planks have been ravaged by nearly a century of ice-grit blasting

these penguins have signed no such pledge. Whereever we go, we are being followed and watched, even talked to in guttural little grunts.

A thin shelf of ice juts out precariously over the water for much of the inner shoreline of Boat Harbour. From above, it looks deceptively safe, yet from below it is a delicate crust, fringed with icicles. It's a miracle that it even supports the weight of the penguins which cluster tentatively near the edge,

How old does a rubbish dump need to be before it becomes an artefact scatter?

daring each other to be the first to take the plunge. They seem so reluctant to dive in that I wonder how they ever find the courage to swim out to the pack in search of krill dinners for themselves and their chicks.

Mawson's hut is a significant feature of the immediate landscape, and we make our way steadily towards its presence. Its appearance is already familiar to us from books and photographs, yet its physical nearness is a thrill. It seems smaller than we had expected. We've also pledged not to go too near the hut, so we wander around its perimeter, amazed to see a midden of rusty relics scattered on the exposed rock surfaces to its north. Rubbish everywhere – boots, leather, seal skins, rusty cans, broken glass, wooden crates, even lumps of coal. All probably once buried deep in snow, emerging only once a year for all to see.

An 'Artefact Scatter' is the official term for this ninety-year-old refuse heap. To an archaeologist it is a gold mine, containing so many examples of long-gone technology, of a lifestyle lived by expeditioners of the heroic era of polar discovery.

Mawson's hut was abandoned in early 1914 and temporarily used as a field hut by French parties from Port Martin in the early fifties. In the seventies, there came a fresh Australian interest in saving the main hut. Several expeditions were sent down over the next three decades to remove vast quantities of packed snow and to assess the extent of weathering. Conservators, archaeologists and heritage carpenters all reported back

A Weddell seal, camouflaged as a rock, takes only a passing interest in our intrusion

with possible strategies. Eventually the non-governmental Mawson's Huts Foundation was formed.

With heritage buildings there is always a debate over whether to rebuild or to simply preserve the remains. Restoration returns them to their original look, but replaces many old materials with new. The Foundation eventually settled on a policy of essentially stabilising things in their current state, locking in the ravages of ninety years of blizzards. The key exception was the re-roofing programme which was just in time to prevent a disastrous acceleration of internal destruction. All but one of the small outbuildings were to be left as standing ruins. And the Foundation is now working in cooperation with the Australian Antarctic Division to achieve its goals.

From our laymen's viewpoint, viewing Mawson's hut from outside was as if we had stepped back into that heroic era ourselves.

1830 HRS
Weddell seals lie like giant slugs on excrement-stained ice as we follow the shoreline past the hut towards the east. They lie in that indeterminate stage between consciousness and sleep, one eye occasionally opening, but lacking the willpower or physical ability to stir more than a flipper as we skirt around them. Their subtle stripings of brown and fawn make them nearly indistinguishable from the half exposed rocks nearby, quite unlike our garishly bright red and yellow outer garments.

Magnetograph House, the only other intact structure, is built without iron nails

Ben has been carrying his cross-country skis, and as we reach the top of the first ridge to the east, he straps them on. This is his idea of bliss. Magnetograph House, not much bigger than a garden shed, stands on this ridge, the lower half of its walls buttressed with piled up rocks. From our reading we know that this is where those early polar heroes gathered data to help locate the elusive South Magnetic Pole, which was miles away to the south-east in those days. The roof has been replaced with authentic looking baltic pine – like the main hut – but we marvel at the weathered planks on the south wall. It's as if it has been grit-blasted for ninety years leaving only a few millimetres of heavily grained timber as a memorial. Almost true, except that the grit was in the form of ice particles, and would have occurred only during the short period of each year that it was not protected by drifts of snow. Without those drifts, the structure would surely have been shredded decades ago

We continue into the next valley where a tiny white field hut and even smaller red dome hut can be seen. Curiosity takes over and we work our way across for a look. Ben's map shows this as Sorenson's hut, a base for the preservation teams which are intermittently sent down. We peer in the window and see a small mess-room with an attached kitchen. No bunk-room except the little red dome. What really catches our attention is the number of wire-ropes, like rigging on a yacht, stropping both structures down to the surrounding rock. This place must really see some wind.

Matt and Ben doing what they love doing

Sorensen's hut , a tiny field base for archaeologists and heritage carpenters

So many photographic opportunities. Such unexpected and unfamiliar scenes. So many shapes of ice and rock. Such a feeling of achievement and wonder. Before we know, it is nearly nine oclock, yet it seems like early afternoon. The sun is still high in the sky, but it's time for us to re-group, eat and talk. And Ben has a sched to keep.

While Ben goes off rowing ...   ... I talk to Barbara on the sat-phone

2100 HRS

Back at *Snow Petrel* it is an idyllic scene. After dinner Ben goes for a short row in our glassy calm little harbour. The cockpit thermometer reads six degrees centigrade, quite a mild afternoon really. Matt goes aloft to shoot more film. And I extricate the sat-phone from its waterproof wrappings for a chat to Barbara.

She's been listening at all our scheds of course, and we've talked briefly on the airwaves, but this is the first private conversation we've had since leaving. She's thrilled for us and has lots of questions over details, how certain things have worked, how the boys have been and what really happened in the knockdown. There are bushfires in Tasmania – something I can't even comprehend in this setting. Neither of us wants to stop talking, but at four dollars a minute we must.

The conversation has been yet another surreal moment. Here I am, anchored in a sheltered bay with the boys playing in the dinghy or up the mast – just like many scenes over the past decades. And I'm talking to Barbara by telephone, for heavens sake, to my wife who's sitting in the cockpit of our boat in a Tasmanian heatwave. Mawson would be turning in his grave.

Sir Douglas Mawson was an enterprising character. His motivation was not purely scientific. Part of his sponsorship brief required him to investigate the commercial potential of this frozen coastline. Conservation issues were not really a part of the psyche of the heroic era of exploration. This is evident from the quantity of local fauna which were slaughtered for the pot – Elephant seals, Weddell seals, hundreds of penguins. Until the realities of the local weather sunk in, Mawson even had high hopes for a future shore-based whaling station to be set up at Cape Denison.

Early twentieth century technology had just embraced Marconi's new invention, the wireless telegraph. Mawson intended to be the first polar explorer to use it to advantage. Radios in those early days were little more than sophisticated crystal sets with a limited range, so an intermediary station was established at Macquarie Island en route south, to receive and relay messages onwards to Australia.

Unfortunately, despite his meticulous planning and a giant aerial erected behind the main hut, not a single message was successfully sent in the first year. However during the second – unplanned – winter at the hut there was some success, and Mawson was able to communicate with his beloved fiancée via a morse code relay. A far cry from my easy sat-phone conversation.

DAY TWO: 20 JANUARY
0400 HRS

Matt, in a fit of artistic enthusiasm, has uncharacteristically decided to get up super early to film a video time sequence of the morning sun climbing from behind the plateau.

This requires someone – me of course – to set an alarm and wake him, then when he's ready, to crawl out of my sleeping bag and help launch the tinker. Naturally I then feel duty-bound to stay up and check that he makes it ashore, with the inevitable requirement of locating and passing various items of last-minute-nearly-forgotten-items down to him before he leaves. The water around us is like a millpond but the air is mighty cold.

They say what goes round comes round, and it's true. I remember my father doing the same for me, slightly grumpily, when I was a lad heading off in the yacht's dinghy for dawn fishing forays in the Marlborough Sounds.

Two hours later, he's back. The sun has never quite escaped a cloud which has crept equally slowly above the skyline. He's tired and rather cross, crawling back into his bag not to emerge until after midday.

0900 HRS

I manage to coax Ben into intermittent consciousness with the cuppa-tea-against-the-face-down-cheek-sipped-between-dozes routine. He's sleeping in the cave again, as there are only two other bunks. I'm keen to go exploring

The view from the tinker — we make the most of settled weather

while it remains flat calm. The barometer is high and steady for the moment which is amazing luck for us.

I'd like to take some photographs from the islet just outside the entrance to Boat Harbour, looking in. If even a moderate katabatic breeze kicks in, it will be asking too much of our two horse outboard to get us back in. And I've experienced the futility of rowing an inflatable against the wind before now.

So Ben and I go for an expedition by sea. Matt managed to break the tinker's seat this morning, leaping in heavily to flee a terrifying little Weddell seal. Ben's a bit dark about that, but we jam a bucket under it as a temporary repair. Both of us would love to get out to the ice-capped island group which sits invitingly a couple of miles offshore, but commonsense prevails despite the tantalisingly calm sea. So we set ourselves the goal of exploring the shoreline to the immediate west. This is the part of Cape Denison where the exposed rock promontory curves back inward to Land's End and rejoins the endless icecliffs.

The outboard, when it starts, is an intrusion of noise, and we throttle it back as low as possible to quieten its impact. Idling our way through tinkling particles of brash, we both are wondering how much abuse the flimsy neoprene skin will tolerate, and whether the aluminium propeller will cope with the task of eggbeating a bowl of icecubes. But after a while without the hiss of a sudden deflation or the abrupt change in engine note of a broken sheer-pin, we relax and enjoy the surrounding spectacle.

All around the shoreline, delicate ice overhangs jutted out across the water

Even out here we can't escape the curiosity of our little Adélie friends. They perch on miniature bergs, flapping at us and staring. Whole flocks of them fly through the water towards us, porpoising under and over the surface at surprising speeds. They seem like an entirely different creature in their watery element, fast and agile, so unlike those clumsy little fat things on land.

Ben hugs the shoreline, ever cautious. Not that either of us expects a sudden rush of wind, but it's nice to know that we are within a stone's-throw of land should anything go wrong. The view from this new location is stunning. There are such subtleties of light and shade. I'm cursing that I didn't take more care listening to Matt's lesson yesterday on exposure settings. Always in the past I've relied on the automatic ability of the camera to look after me. But now with so much reflected light, I'm trying to manipulate the settings to avoid underexposure of the details I'm trying to capture. And this is my last roll of slow film.

For Mawson's team, this promontory of exposed rock was their entire world for a very long time. It is an interesting reflection of Australia's links with the mother country in that era, that this largely Australian group of men named their accessible extremities 'Land's End' and 'John O'Groats' – named after the equivalent north-south extremes of Great Britain. The span between these locations is a mere three kilometres, but for much of the winter, even that short distance would have been impossible to cover.

Some of Hurley's photographic plates illustrate the exertion required to walk against such a solid mass of fast-moving dense air. 'Wind-walking', they called it, and the sepia fur-clad human images appear to defy gravity as they lean into the wind at a seemingly impossible angle.

1400 HRS

We're on board *Snow Petrel* again, and Matt is stirring in his bunk. I'm eager for Matt to get some video footage of the tinker idling through brash. Ben's seen enough though and wants to potter on board, tidying up the rigging, and splicing stronger wire strops for the shore-lines. None of us can believe how mild it is with the sun high in the sky and not a breath of wind. It reminds me of those days when we used to pile all five boys into our Cortina wagon for a sunny day in the Mount Ruapehu snow.

So Matt and I begin retracing the track of the morning's expedition, lingering indulgently to video long sequences of penguins competing for space on the little bergs. We slowly work our way down the western side of the promontory again to the spectacular giant face at Land's End. It is an enormous overhanging ice cliff, its sheer face exposing layers of grey moraine which have been trapped during the thousands of years it has taken to reach this final truncation.

I drop Matt off on a low isolated rock which lies nearly awash about fifty metres offshore. Then I cruise quietly in below the overhang for Matt to record the scale of this enormous feature. Suddenly I am seized with a sense of danger. Any of the precarious overhangs could let go far above me in an instant, triggered by the sound of this outboard or perhaps a shout from Matt. In the space of a few seconds, I would be engulfed in ice in full view of Matt before he too would be engulfed – in his case by an enormous pressure wave which like a sub-zero tsunami would sweep him to oblivion.

Gingerly I manoeuvre my way back to him and seize him reluctantly aboard. He hasn't quite filmed the sequence he wanted, but seeing the look in my eyes, he doesn't argue.

Don and Margie MacIntyre know Cape Denison more intimately than anyone alive. They sailed down on two large yachts in the nineties, and spent 1995 living in a home-built temporary hut near Mawson's Magnetograph House. The emotional deprivation and extreme physical battering they experienced – despite modern technology – were recorded in 'Two Below Zero'.

Ben already knew them from his stint as first mate on their ice-strengthened small ship Sir Hubert Wilkins. *We were hauled out on the*

The giant overhangs at Land's End dwarfed me in the tinker

Kettering slipway when the rumour-mill reached them, and they were down in a flash, offering equipment, encouragement and advice. For Barbara it was a turning point to hear what they had to say. For me too. Suddenly the trip seemed something achievable, as if a layer of mystery had been peeled away to expose the practical reality beneath.

As the Cape Denison gurus, they had been head-hunted to organise a voyage back down for a hundred tourists on the ice-strengthened ship Orion. *And they were due to arrive on 21 January.*

1700 HRS

It's Ben's turn to be grumpy. He's determined to create a good impression for Don and Margie tomorrow. 'This ship's a tip,' he grumbles, conveniently ignoring the fact that much of the mess is of his own making. Good humouredly we set about tidying up, until Matt decides he needs to be ferried ashore with his tripod to photograph the view from the moraine line high above Mawson's hut. He claims the sun is at the right angle, but naturally we rib him about his excuse to avoid work. Ben's in good spirits again and together we tease Matt unmercifully while I repair the tinker seat.

Ben has spliced up some really professional looking wire strops for our shore-lines to replace the temporary bulldog clamps he used when we arrived. He doesn't admit it but I know that he is primarily motivated by the desire to have things looking ship-shape and Bristol fashion tomorrow. After all, Don is a famous yachtsman. Those multiple bulldog clamps would have held us in any storm.

2100 HRS

Ben's having a very full sched tonight. Several calls from other yachting friends and a talk to Don on board *Orion*. Ben gives Don the waypoints of the break in the pack we had located in case *Orion* can adjust the drift factor and nudge her way in. Don is relieved to hear that the Mawson's hut western door isn't buried in snow, and gives us a tentative ETA of 0900 tomorrow. Meanwhile Mike Harris has some less than good news. The High just north of us will be dissipating soon, as a deep Low sweeps in. It seems that our luck is about to change.

We decide to get to bed before midnight so that our biorhythms can readjust. There's a breeze puffing up and Ben makes the last minute call to heave the tinker back on deck for the night – just in case. We drift off to sleep with balaclavas over our eyes to block out the light.

DAY THREE: 21 JANUARY

0300 HRS

It was a good call of Ben's. I wake to the whistling and clanking of a solid 45 knot southerly in the rig. It's nice to lie in bed knowing that everything is secure, and there's no need to drag myself out. It's bitterly cold in the cabin, and my hot water bottle is still warm.

1200 HRS

We've had the VHF on since eight but not a squeak from *Orion*. Outside, the wind has slowly eased back to 25 knots. It's a relief as we aren't psychologically ready for a full-blown katabatic gale, and we know how important today's visit is to Don and Margie. The barometer has stabilised and we think the overnight wind may be part of the regular daily cycle of katabatic drainage during stable weather. It's quite cloudy today and is still freezing in the cabin. Ben even lit his little diesel heater for a while to take the edge out of the cold in here.

We spend a pleasant hour watching some of Matt's video footage in the viewfinder. He's been having some problems with the camcorder flashing a condensation message and not working. It would be a pity for it to break down now in the midst of these unprecedented footage opportunities. While he waits for it to settle down, he ventures up into the cold to photograph the sea-spray icicles which have clustered along the exposed sections of bow-lines.

After three hours of waiting we're getting bored. The wind has backed and eased to a light easterly. Ben packs the hand-held VHF in his day-bag and

Erected to commemorate
the supreme sacrifice made by
Lieut. B.E.S. Ninnis, R.F. and
Dr. X. Mertz in the cause of science
A.A.E. 1913
A.J. Hodgeman

The cross on Azimuth Hill, a stark reminder of the risks taken in that heroic era

we head for the shore again. All of us are aware that today might be our last chance to visit Memorial Cross, and from Azimuth Hill we may even see if *Orion* is approaching.

We linger for some time at the cross. I even find myself speaking in hushed tones. It's not a religious experience but a reflective one. The monument seems to have an atmosphere about it quite unlike the other structures we've been near. Somehow it seems to imbue a sense of solemnity, and I can picture the men as they erected it, over ninety years ago. It was their tribute to the two men they had spent nearly a year of intimate cohabitation with, in a relentless battle with the elements.

Ben and Matt are less reflective. Ben is more interested in how the timber has weathered, and how it has been recently repaired. Matt is soon off, photographing the fluffy Adélie chicks in one of the dozens of colonies just below us. There is no sign of a ship anywhere out to sea.

The story behind this tragedy is well known in Australian history, and legendary as a feat of polar survival. Douglas Mawson set off on 10 November 1912 after a winter's preparations, on a sledging journey with two dog sledges and two companions, Belgrade Ninnis and Xavier Mertz, the dog handler. They were mapping King George V Land – as the hinterland had been named – pushing inland to the east as far as possible in an agreed time span. Their supply ship Aurora *was due to collect the entire team in mid January, and the weather had already delayed their departure.*

They had covered 315 miles and were crossing the second huge glacier on 14 December when Ninnis disappeared down a snow-covered crevasse along with the sledge which carried the tent and most of the food rations. For Ninnis and his six dogs the final seconds would probably have equated to falling down a hundred storey stairwell.

Mertz and Mawson now had to backtrack the huge distance with inadequate shelter and only ten days' food. They resorted to eating the dogs, a necessary betrayal which virtually broke Mertz's heart. He was semi-vegetarian and his dogs were his close buddies. It is generally accepted that when he died three weeks later he had succumbed to Vitamin A poisoning as a result of overdosing on dog livers. A recent medical study challenges this though, claiming that his metabolism was less able to cope with the carnivorous diet and psychological stress associated with the systematic slaughter of his beloved dogs.

For the shattered Mawson, his friend's slow and horrible death ironically boosted his own survival as, without the need to share, there were now sufficient remaining meagre rations to keep him going until he reached a pre-excavated ice-cave food cache not far from Cape Denison. He finally struggled back to the main hut to see Aurora *sailing away, and be met by a small band of volunteers committed to over-wintering a second year in the slim chance of the expedition's return. It was this small group of volunteers who worked with him to erect the cross.*

1700 HRS

We are aboard with a hot drink when Don's voice suddenly booms in on the VHF. He hopes to anchor at six and depart at midnight. The pack was far too dense and nearly had them licked, he says, obviously impressed that we had managed to find a way through. He's clearly anxious about the speed of operations needed, so Ben volunteers our assistance.

Our first task, after a hasty baked beans dinner, is to weight our western bow-line down under the surface so that the big tenders can get past us. Don has asked that one of us stays aboard in case more lines need juggling, so I volunteer. Meanwhile I run the boys ashore to locate a suitable landing site and cut some steps with our two ice-axes.

It's a very slick operation. Don and several staff wave out to me as the first black tender cruises purposefully past *Snow Petrel*. Nudging up to the boys' landing spot, they rapidly disgorge barrels and boxes of emergency supplies barely in time to receive guests from the next two boats not far behind. From my vantage point in the cockpit I see a fluid mass of red figures fanning out across the whiteness as the black boats continue their shuttling. One incoming tender veers towards me and I recognise Margie's cheerful round face beaming at me through her yellow shell garments and hat. She tosses me a package and mimes a big hug as the tender continues on its way. 'From Barb,' she shouts above the purr of the big diesel outboard.

Unexpectedly the breeze swings briefly to the north. Immediately the starboard aft stern-line pulls tight on the surface like a road barrier. Exactly what we'd promised Don would not happen. I do a quick fix with another weight and feed out some more slack before settling back aboard with a discreet pair of binoculars to watch the action. At the landing I can see Ben and Matt helping passengers out of the shuttle boats, completely at ease in this different role. Their people-skills have kicked back in again and I'm proud of them. It's as if we have become temporary custodians of this special place, welcoming more special people who will value it too. Considering the money they must have spent getting here, I'm sure they all will.

I begin opening the package to see three pairs of thick fleece lined freezer gloves and a letter from Barbara. Special delivery! Mawson will be getting positively restless tonight.

A shout from alongside startles me out of my reverie. It's Ben in the bow of one of the black tenders, almost as big as *Snow Petrel*. The diesel outboard purrs so quietly that I didn't even hear it. He sings out for me to come ashore, and I climb aboard. The wind has swung back to the south now and is rapidly freshening. The evening katabatic drainage maybe? Or does that darkening sky spell something more sinister?

Once ashore I find myself unexpectedly enjoying this return to human contact. I take over from the boys who are keen to take up an invitation to visit the ship. The invitation was for me too of course, but I've declined in favour of the opportunity to see inside Mawson's hut later before it's sealed up again.

These rock and snow improvised steps at the landing are already freezing badly as the wind becomes a blast-freezer. There's a flow of elderly passengers returning to the warmth and comfort of their floating hotel. They have boot chains clipped to their shoes and many need a hand with lifejackets. Most have a look of near elation on their frozen faces, but there's always an exception. 'Did you enjoy that?' – my standard query. She's a tight-lipped old battle-axe this one. 'Been there done that' … So there's the rub. Money doesn't always buy happiness.

Visitors from *Orion* briefly interrupt our solitude

The advantage of working with some of the staff here is that I can hear the radio chat from the hand-held in Belinda's pocket. In particular, Don's voice crackling out queries and instructions. He sounds tense and I don't blame him. He has a huge responsibility and this wind is rapidly building. There's a concern being expressed about the sea conditions for the tenders. He's ordering a general recall to the ship, earlier than planned, like a colonel sounding a retreat. It will take time though, with the number of shuttles shared between the three big black people-movers.

For me though there's enough time to join the last of the queue outside the hut. I've barely reached it when a strong Kiwi accent greets me, attached to a familiar face. It takes a moment to connect the face to a name but he helps me out. Rob Schuster had once spent a summer in New Zealand's sub-antarctic islands on a sea-lion research trip with our son, Dan. At the time, Dan had been our southern adventurer. How the tables have turned.

Entering the hut entails squeezing through an excavated tunnel of compacted snow. It's dark inside, just a few torches. The skylights all have shutters now. I soon hear Ben and Matt's voices, and am thrilled that they've returned in time for this unique experience. Diane, the officially sanctioned

Evidence of the lifestyle of Mawson's men is obvious everywhere inside the hut

guide, can't waste too much time but we have nearly ten minutes to soak up the magic of the place. Its unique smells, the ice crystals which sparkle on the walls like a scene from Dr Zhivago's winter residence, the intact shelves of books and food containers. Even the pictures on Mawson's cubicle wall. One six-penny book which catches my eye is labelled 'To Pleasure Madame'. In 1912 it was probably advice about pipesmoke, slippers and husbandly duties, but the mind does boggle nevertheless. My speculations are interrupted by Don's urgent crackle on Diane's VHF. It's imperative that the last guests return immediately. Apparently one of the huge people-movers has nearly flipped during its unladen return to shore.

As tail-enders, we return to the landing-steps in time to help a chain-gang effort of reloading the emergency gear into the last boat. The wind has reached gale force now and Don is tense. Even the ship has begun to drag its anchor out there. It's only the staff on board for this final shuttle, and they drop us back to *Snow Petrel* with a flood of good will.

Then they're off, and we're alone once more.

I had never experienced the logistical demands of a big tourist operation until this trip. Naturally back in my Outdoor Education days there had been teens to organise and check, but not on the scale seen here. The protocols and responsibilities involved in disembarking a hundred often frail tourists into such an alien environment are enormous.

IAATO is the umbrella organisation which encompasses much of the tourism on the continent, most of which occurs on the more accessible Peninsula, thousands of miles from Cape Denison. Apart from two Russian icebreakers which had visited once or twice over the past decade, Orion was one of very few tourist ships ever to have strayed this far. It is a long way from New Zealand or Australia for a very small visitable area, unless some sub-antarctic islands, the French base or maybe the Ross Sea can be included.

The environmental protocols involve issues like boot-sterilising, limiting proximity to fauna, and of course the egg disposal. These constraints are spelled out aboard the ships before disembarkation. Special character zones like this one have further limitations designed to protect heritage artefacts. Nothing may be removed, whether of human or natural origin. Entry to historic sites like Mawson's huts may only be done in restricted numbers under the supervision of an approved guide. Regulations are set for Cape Denison by Australian legislation and overseen by the Antarctic Division.

Don and Margie MacIntyre. They have spent more time at Cape Denison than anyone alive

Then there are the duty of care issues. Risk management procedures. Limiting tourists ashore to a set number, like one hundred, is an example. The tangible signs for us were the boxes and barrels. Enough tent shelters to house everyone who landed. And enough supplies to feed them. That was the bottom line. It would have been Don's worst nightmare to have had to use them of course. And that's where his judgement call came in.

2230 HRS

It's strange to be just the three of us once more, after experiencing such a flood of humanity. The boys are buzzing. Their trip out to *Orion* was a success in more ways than one. They managed to take our entire fortnight's rubbish with them to the ship, have a luxury shower each, eat half a buffet in the company of two exciting Sydney girls, and return loaded with luxury provisions. Ben can't wait to show me.

I produce Barbara's parcel first and we finish opening it. The freezer gloves are fantastic. Much better than our woollen-gloves-in-rubber-garden-glove combo we've been using. She's found us a really good bird identification book and for Ben's failing wet weather gear she's sent some waterproofing spray. It's like Christmas all over again.

Ben starts handing down items from the big *Orion* food parcel next. I'm in heaven when I see loaves of sliced bread. There are venison sausages, frozen veges, three melons, three bottles of classy wine and (Matt's eyes sparkling) a whole slab of beer. We eat melon washed down with beer while the boys speculate on how their liaisons aboard may have developed if the captain hadn't packed them off in mid-meal with dire warnings of a rising gale. Their description of the surging re-embarkation and wild ride back to shore helps explain Don's obvious agitation.

The tinker is well lashed down on the foredeck before we wriggle into our sleeping bags. Outside, the whistling has gone up an octave.

Ice build-up in *Snow Petrel*'s rigging

PHASE 6

The Elements Are Unleashed

In his fascinating book, 'Ice', Tristran Jones describes the effect of enforced idleness during the time he spent frozen into the Arctic sea-ice. He was beset aboard his converted lifeboat Cresswell *for two winters with only his one-eyed dog, Nelson, for company. He writes about how he played chess against himself, dividing his mind into two separate individuals – each jealously guarding his intentions from the other.*

The effects on his metabolism are revealed in his claim to have been able to look at his clock and see the minute hand moving quite quickly around the dial. The hour-hand would be steadily creeping between each number. Perhaps even human physiology is capable of entering a semi-hibernation phase.

DAY FOUR: 22 JANUARY
0930 HRS

I feel like a big seal myself now, dozing the hours away in my envelope of warmth. But my toes hurt, a constant tingling sting of inflamed tissue around the toenails – the consequence of too many inactive night watches in cold rubber boots.

Without even opening my eyes, I'm aware of a sustained pitch of shrieking wind outside. I've lived with incessant wind before, for several years at Chaffer's Marina in downtown Wellington, but this has a much deeper resonance. It doesn't rise and fall with the gusts and squalls of normal gales. It's a solid constant rush of dense snow-laden air. With my eyes still closed, I guess the wind-speed from the pitch. Eighty knots maybe? This sub-zero air is so much denser than anything I've experienced.

There's no point getting up so I doze a while. But my bladder is complaining, and I'm curious. The incessant shriek has set my adrenaline off. It's ten o'clock and the cabin thermometer reads minus two. The portapot pump has frozen up and I scrape the ice from inside the galley window to peer out. It's a spectacular look. Ice-encrusted staunchions and shrouds, snow-covered decks, and beyond that a frenzy of white streaked waves far larger than could possibly be generated in the hundred-odd metre fetch from land. Beyond that, no land , nothing but a mist of white particles rushing past at unbelievable speed. Surely we can't have dragged our way out of the inlet?

Alarmed, I poke my head into the dome. Nothing but white. Of course, it's snowed up, stupid. Opening the hatch, I peer into a flurry of swirling powder. At least now there's the comfort of two sternlines stretching away in a wind-tensioned arc to some point beyond the flying frozen spray. We're holding.

Ben has stirred for my report. He has no doubts about our security of course. His splices are bulletproof. But he's reluctant to light the diesel heater. Uses too much valuable diesel and anyway the flue won't draw. So I run the engine for some heat and make a cup of tea for the two of us, then wriggle back into the warmth of my sleeping bag after a brief panic that I've lost my reading glasses.

1300 HRS

Matt stirs at last. The photographer in him has finally overcome the seal. He scoffs down some cereal and a couple of partly refrozen slices of our new bread, then takes twenty minutes to kit himself out in five layers of thermal gear. I lend him Barbara's little waterproof snapshot camera and he's off. Within a minute he's back for a facemask and a pair of our new freezer gloves. He's frozen and can hardly talk, and before he ventures back outside he spends half an hour swaddling his camcorder in plastic bags for some blizzard footage.

It's interesting how we're adopting the behaviours of the other local creatures. The penguins, like the seals, spend a large proportion of their time here lying around or in a huddle, taking random turns to venture out on a

Nowhere could escape the ingress of snow as 100 knot winds swept past

foray somewhere. It must be a primeval instinct to conserve energy. Matt returns from his intrepid foray, bringing clumps of snow in with him which very slowly melt on the floor from the slight warmth of the engine. He peels off his layers and crawls back into his bunk to thaw out. He's excited about his footage and is bemoaning the fact that we can't launch the tinker for footage of *Snow Petrel* in a blizzard.

Out at sea Orion *was away from the effect of katabatic downflow, which rushes down the slopes, slowing a few miles offshore like a playground slide levelling at the bottom. Instead the ship was battling a 75 knot easterly blizzard associated with the Low, and dodging thick pack ice. The captain had to hand-steer for twenty one hours.*

At our location, slap in the middle of both influences, we were experiencing the combination of air being both pushed and pulled – from high pressure inland towards low pressure out at sea. The southerly katabatic winds were being wrenched eastward as they reached us.

So we were experiencing this wind as a sou'easterly, attacking us from our port bow. Ben's strategy of running an extra port side breastline was a good one. The effect on Snow Petrel *was an induced heel to starboard, especially in any extreme gusts.*

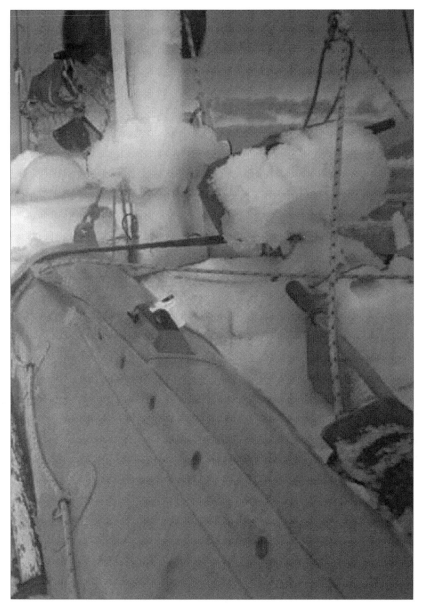

As over a ton of ice built up on deck, our galley sink began to backfill alarmingly

1700 HRS

The degree of ice build-up is becoming alarming. We can feel the roll becoming progressively more sluggish as the mast and rigging turn into thickening columns of ice. Much of it is sea-ice as sheets of water lift off the surface and freeze onto anything metal.

Ben is the next to gather the will-power to venture outside. He's keen to check for chafe, but staggers back in very quickly to report on a huge build-up of ice protruding from our starboard topsides and a miniature iceberg growing around our anchor chain. We are sitting deeper in the water too under the weight of a ton or more of ice. In the galley there is clear evidence of this. The sink is partly backfilling as the plug-hole lowers below the outside water-level.

I put off facing the extreme wind-chill for as long as my curiosity allows. We are all guessing wind strengths, as Ben has no anemometer on *Snow Petrel*. If we had the appropriate tables, we could probably calculate an average speed from the ratio of wave heights to our fetch.

Outside at last, I drink in the scene. The waves are racing past at over half a metre high, constantly overtaken at incredible speed by flying frozen scud. It's really hard to breathe, even with my face covered. Two minutes is as long as I can manage. My gloved fingers refuse to push the trigger on Barbara's little green camera, so I make do with knocking the frozen sheath off the VHF aerial on the pushpit. The ice build-up there is as thick as my wrist and the skinny little aerial is threatening to self-destruct under the combined onslaught of wind pressure and weight.

Now that the elements were truly unleashed, we had time to reflect on how fortunate we had been, during our final preparations, to have such generous and supportive friends. Once Ben's plans had become more widely known we received offers of clothing, equipment and even freeze-dried food rations. The MacIntyres were the first, but before long other good friends had us kitted in quality gear including goggles, shell garments and even spare ice-axes. Admittedly I still had to make do with gumboots and multiple layers of socks, but we left with far better gear than our small budget would otherwise have allowed.

And as we lay in our icy cabin with the blizzard shrieking outside, it was not just the physical equipment we were grateful for, but the bucketful of goodwill that accompanied each gift or loan.

2100 HRS

There is simply no let-up to this blizzard. We've been trying to guess the strength of its fury. Back in New Zealand we would know when the wind exceeded 70 knots. The williwaws would lift clouds of spray high into the air. But Mawson regularly measured over 150 knots so we are beginning to agree that this blizzard could be conservatively in the vicinity of a hundred, especially whenever the roar outside reaches a deeper resonating vibration.

For days we idled away the hours ...   ... the little diesel heater occasionally
                                              warming our cabin

The pipe to the galley pump has frozen solid. I'm desperate for some heat and at last Ben begins to relent. With two empty baked bean cans, I cut and bend a venturi flue cap for the diesel heater. The old cap was broken off in the knockdown and we've had a plastic bottle taped on ever since. Once it's jammed securely on and Ben has fired it up, the cabin temperature slowly rises to a wonderful eight degrees, assisted by the soy mince curry which Ben cooks up for dinner.

Warm tummies and warm fingers. We block out the battering elements above us with the distractions of a wine cask, peanuts and cards. Simple pleasures prevail till midnight.

DAY FIVE: 23 JANUARY
1400 HRS

Time has become irrelevant in these circumstances. Lying in our warm cocoons there is no motivation to stir. Everlasting filtered light gives no indication of whether it is night or day. I've been aware of my stinging toes and numb soles between dozing, and of an incessant roar outside with a muted jerking motion. The jerks confirm the security of our cats' cradle of lines outside.

But a new noise has me puzzled. A random crash and scrape above my head. Curiosity and the craving for a cup of tea finally get the better of me. Once the kettle is charged with water from a bottle I open the hatch for a preview. Some sort of thaw is apparent despite the shrieking wind. Big chunks of ice are crashing from the rigging onto the deck and skidding rapidly aft. Icicles hanging from the solar panels are dripping steadily. The cockpit is still full of snow, even the dodger, but the sky has turned blue and the sun has emerged. The wind may still be storm-force, but the air is no longer full of driving snowflakes.

What do you call a 3 pm breakfast? Ours is a strange one. Porridge and maple syrup followed by semi-frozen curry on toast. Matt and Ben are now competing for books. Ben's a lightning fast reader, always has been. We used to call him E.T. – input input … The problem is that Matt is reading a six book fantasy series and is half way through book three. Ben started the same series yesterday and has just finished book two. So now they're taking turns with the same book and making do with something else in the off-time. I'm reading 'My Old Man and the Sea' about a father and son who sailed around Cape Horn together in a tiny 26 footer.

We read on. Occasionally someone pokes their head out for a brief look around, or even kits up for an expedition on deck to club the ice-encrusted rigging. The 1830 hr weather fax doesn't happen because the radio refuses to warm up in time. Matt is back-viewing his entire video footage so we crowd around the tiny screen for the good bits, especially the pack ice sequence. It's our version of an evening's TV – the Discovery Channel, weirdly inverted onto us.

Books were a big part of all the boys' childhoods. Our fortnightly visit to the library was an important occasion. Our boys probably wore out the Arthur Ransome series. By ten, Ben had graduated from children's fiction to adult non-fiction, but didn't yet have the social judgement to differentiate between appropriate and spurious. His teacher once contacted us over the content of a Tristran Jones' autobiographical tale. The navy ditties and brothel references didn't seem quite suitable for his age.

2000 HRS

I ring Barbara on the sat-phone. We talked faintly by radio last night but I missed most of what she said. Domestic details of insurance and finances are the most urgent, but it's so nice just to talk privately, to re-enter each other's space emotionally if not physically. It's hard to stop.

Matt cooks another fantastic soup for dinner which we wash down with more cask wine. Nobody feels that we should open any of the four bottles from the cupboard above my bunk. We settle into a game of rummy from eleven till one, but I can't sleep after that. It's still broad daylight and my feet are frozen. Instead I read George Orwell's '1984' from cover to cover, pausing midway to heat up a hottie for my feet. It's a struggle turning the pages with gloved fingers.

When I finish at five, Matt is partially awake, changing the CD in his walkman. His feet are bothering him too.

DAY SIX: 24 JANUARY
1400 HRS

Well! We realise now how lucky we were to arrive when we did. I'm cooking porridge and it's howling outside. But it has abated to about 45 knots, gusting 60. And the barometer is rising.

The water tanks have frozen solid, and we're trying to keep a spare water-container on the floor, sufficiently thawed to use a short hose direct to the galley pump. Meanwhile we keep water bottles near our bunks where they are less likely to freeze. I make the effort to shovel snow out of the cockpit leaving enough to bury the *Orion* frozen veges. The danger of iced-up rigging has largely gone now, as most of the large columns of ice have thawed in the sun's radiant energy despite the continuing wind and spray.

We all spend the rest of the afternoon in bed reading. Ben has overtaken Matt now, reading through the night, and is half way through book four.

1800 HRS

Lunch, a late bacon and eggs treat (shells into a bag of course). It's a chance for us all to talk a while. But the mood is one of introversion. I put on an 'Offspring' CD to show Matt I don't hate punk rock.

Music became almost as important as food during this incarcerated phase. Before we sailed from Tasmania we had all selected some favourite CDs for the player. I plumped for universal albums like Pink Floyd, Paul Kelly, Waterboys and Dire Straits. Ben chose various Techno albums, Oasis (a carryover from his time studying in England), and various nineties music. Matt is an avid Punk rocker, and had some terrible versions of what had originally been nice music. But there were some notable exceptions...

2100 HRS

Tonight's sched has some disturbing news. It's third hand from Mike and originated from Don MacIntyre on *Orion* via satellite email to Barbara. Apparently there is now a band of seven-tenths to ten-tenths ice, sixty miles thick, cutting off our escape route north. It extends for at least eighty miles to our west, and is the result of the storm force easterlies in this Low. Apparently *Orion* aborted its cruise into the French territory and managed to escape direct from Cape Denison in 75 knot winds before the door slammed shut. Don is advising us to wait at least a week in the hope of southerlies to dissipate the pack, and then check how much build-up there is near the French base.

This turn of events certainly adds a new dimension to cruising these waters, even at this time of year. It's not just a weather window we're looking for, but an ice window too.

We're all a bit depressed tonight. The incessant storm force winds are taking their toll on our morale. We can empathise with Mawson's men putting up with this battering for a year, and also with Don and Margie ten years ago. At least the sun is out, and through thawing windows, we can see Adélie penguins attempting to go about their business. The ones returning from sea are struggling to gain a footing on ice-slicked rocks while those diving in are being showered with icy spray.

Ben's keen to get ashore if it drops to 35 knots or less tomorrow. We need to break into a lake for unfrozen water. And he's still keen to see the snow petrel colony at Land's End.

Too cold and sobered for cards, we wriggle deep into our sleeping bags to read the hours away.

Mawson's book, 'Home of the Blizzard', makes fascinating reading on the psychology of men under the onslaught of persistent hurricane strength winds. His strategy was to keep up a routine of regular tasks and scientific work, peppered with fun occasions for light relief.

He mentions how startled the men became on the rare occasions that the wind lulled. For them the shriek was the norm and the silence an aberration.

DAY SEVEN: 25 JANUARY
1030 HRS

It's the sheer relentlessness of this wind that astounds us. I'm prodded into consciousness by a regular insistent banging somewhere outside near my head. A big lump of ice has formed around a rope hanging over the side and is now thumping regularly against the hull.

The pitch of the wind has notched up nearly an octave again. There's a hollow metallic shriek, and the first day's vibration is back, transmitted down into the hull from the mast. My attempts to fill the kettle for a cup of tea are frustrated. The jerry can which we've been using is now largely frozen solid, despite being on the floor of the galley away from the steel plating. That only leaves the water bottles or melted deck ice.

Matt's sleeping like a baby and I watch him for a while. His twenty-one-year-old unlined face is framed by a thick red stubble which doesn't extend above his upper lip. His placid good-humoured personality shows up even in his sleep. I can almost hear his infectious chuckle as I gaze at him, remembering his birth.

I cried after Matt was born. I don't remember being that emotional after any of the other four births. You would think that having a fifth son would seem like old hat. He was overdue and needed to be induced. Even at that age he loved to sleep in. Barbara had a choice of birthday for him, so she chose the day between mine and Josh's.

We were vaguely hoping for a little girl, but my distinct memory of his birth was another dangling pair of testicles and a plump pink body. But my tears were of the intensity of the occasion, not of sorrow.

He always was a people-person. With so many older brothers, and the experience of having half his entire schooling on correspondence education, he needed to be adaptable and make new friends easily. But despite his easy-going demeanour, he had an inner strength which especially showed up at sea. Even before he reached his teens, he could stand up to adversities which many an adult would baulk at.

When he left home we began to worry that despite his obvious intelligence he was drifting aimlessly through life – even though we under-stood his decision to take up a job serving petrol rather than attend university. Perhaps this trip would help him find a course to steer.

1400 HRS

During porridge, Ben outlines his thinking about our escape route. If the main mass of pack ice has been driven westwards by this storm and has fetched up hard against the ice-shelf past the French territory, then it stands to reason that it will have thinned out to the east. Unless the Ross Sea break-out ice has filled up that area too. So maybe we might try an easterly route out when this eases, sailing towards the Mertz Glacier and exploring northwards for a lead. There's no knowing when a southerly will come to scatter it all again. Katabatics are southerlies, but they don't reach far enough. And within three weeks, the sea will start freezing over for the winter.

I'm getting restless. There's no chance of getting ashore yet. It's going to be another quiet day. But I've got plans to reorganise the galley shelves more efficiently. And then there are the cupboards. They need re-stowing for the trip home. We'll be mostly on port tack, so there are things to move ...

DAY EIGHT: 26 JANUARY
0830 HRS

This is hopefully to be Operation Escape Day. I wake to my alarm, immediately conscious of the shriek of wind in the rigging. I'm not prepared to believe it until I've actually looked at the sea through the dome. The spray is being lifted off the whitecaps as they race past our hull.

I relieve myself and sink back into oblivion.

1200 HRS

A new problem has surfaced. We feel it first as an abrupt sideways jerk on the hull. It doesn't take long to work out what has happened. The shoreline around us has changed completely during this storm. Not a single ice-crust overhang is left. They have all collapsed onto the rocks below and as it nears high tide today they are beginning to float off, blowing straight out of the bay only to be brought up with a jerk by our shorelines. Each time it happens we need to spend ten minutes in the icy wind freeing them up.

1500 HRS

At last, for the first time in nearly five days, the wind has eased to only 35 knots. Matt and Ben gear up for a wet ride ashore in the tinker, sliding along the ice-clad starboard bow-line on a pair of tethers. Before they even begin their ride, a film of ice has formed on the neoprene skin. With them they take two 30-litre plastic barrels and a 20-litre jerry can. They plan to use both ice axes to smash an entry hole into the lake on the ridge above Mawson's hut. We need water in liquid form, to top up the remaining ice in our two hull water tanks.

While they are gone, I check over the engine and replace both bolts on the stuffing box. A couple of hours pass, so I continue shifting things around in the lockers. Once we're heeling again we'll have the problem of

At last a chance to break into a frozen lake to replenish with liquid water

food cans falling out each time we open the uphill windward locker door. I need to finish shifting these across to starboard, the expected new lee side for the trip home.

Out the galley porthole I can see Ben and Matt struggling with the barrels. They've tied ropes to them, but even as I watch, I see Ben lose his footing and slip over. They transfer the water containers to the tinker and cast off the eastern stern-line. Another hour passes while they work their way around to the west to release the stern and breast lines. This keeps me busy coiling away cold ice-encrusted ropes before they return.

It's good to get liquid water back into the tanks but Ben's not satisfied that we have enough. He's sore from several falls and is clearly anxious to get ourselves ready to leave. This time it's Matt and me heading ashore for more water. Matt warns me that the snow crust is lethal but it doesn't look too bad to me. That's until I take the first ten steps – then I see what he means. I begin to regret not bringing crampons. But I'm pleased to get ashore for a last walk, and it's an experience to ladle the crystal clear lake water from the boys' hole into the containers.

2100 HRS

Mike's been very busy for us today. On the sched he confirms a promising break in the weather and we can hear the relief in Ben's voice. Mike has also located an internet source of satellite ice pictures for this area. Apparently it shows a tantalising hint of a break in the pack to our north-east, but only as far as the skies are clear. Thick cloud is blocking the bit we really need to see.

By the time we've finished with water, dinner and stowage it's midnight and the tide is high. That means another fleet of ice-rafts to clear from our lines. At least there are only the two bow-lines left now. And Ben has made his decision. We won't waste precious fuel searching for an elusive eastern lead. No, we'll sail for French territory where we may get expert advice on how the ice is dissipating. And we'll wait until the warmth of the morning's sun. Time to sleep.

The wind is a steady 35 knots still but we're convinced it'll be easing more tomorrow. I set my alarm and we turn in. There's a mood of high anticipation now.

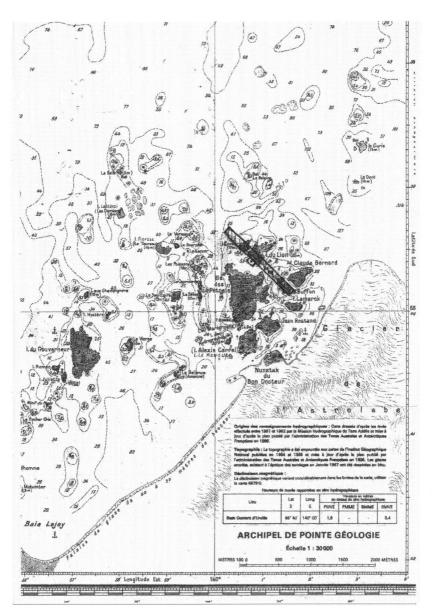

Extract of old French chart No. 6285 - Dumont D'Urville Base and Astrolabe Glacier

PHASE 7

French Territory

My childhood sailing areas were riddled with exotic sounding names: Croisilles Harbour, D'Urville Island, Astrolabe Roadstead, Chicot Rocks; a legacy of the French explorer Dumont D'Urville's visit to New Zealand's South Island in 1827.

One of my favourite teenage destinations, Adele Island, drew its name from the same French lady as the characterful penguins which were now all around us. D'Urville effectively immortalised his wife in this gesture, even naming the Antarctic hinterland 'Terre Adélie' in her honour.

Those gorgeous Tasman Bay waters must have seemed like heaven compared with the bitter cold and danger he found on his square-rigged L'Astrolabe, when he ventured south into Antarctic waters in 1840. The same waters that we were about to sail through as we weighed anchor from Cape Denison.

DAY NINE: 27 JANUARY
0800 HRS

I'm simultaneously aware of my watch-alarm and a whistling in the rig. Not a shrieking – only 35 knots. The sun is beating out of a clear blue sky and the barometer has risen ten millibars overnight.

We gather in the two bow-lines and shorten up the chain to thirty metres. There are still a dozen little details to attend to, and we're concerned about how to turn around in this narrow anchorage with this wind. To our relief, by mid morning it abruptly eases to 15 knots.

Matt seizes the opportunity to rush ashore in the tinker to film our departure but Ben is in no mood to dilly dally. I feel sorry for Matt, struggling to set up his camcorder as we steam straight past him out of the little harbour where Ben waits for him to rejoin us. It's nearly the first full-blown argument of the voyage and takes Matt a while to cool off. Only one extra minute was all he needed for a good piece of footage. Their priorities have diverged and I feel like the piggy in the middle.

1200 HRS

We are bound for Port Martin, a small ice-free promontory and archipelago of islets 40 miles to our east. It will be the first significant break in the ice-cliffs on our way along the coast. And we are shortly to enter the French sector of Antarctica, which is an exciting fresh development for us.

Such a difference from the past five days. We are motor-sailing with a light quartering breeze in brilliant sunlight and comparative warmth. As we work our way a couple of miles offshore the breeze dies away completely, but Ben doesn't complain about the motor this time.

Dumont D'Urville's land claim included Cape Denison, but the Australian and French governments subsequently adjusted the claim as an equivalent sized segment to the west of Mawson's hut.

The French did not set up a base until the late 1940s, establishing it on the headland at Port Martin with field excursions to Cape Denison and Île des Petrels (Pointe Géologie), 40 miles east and west respectively. However the katabatics at Port Martin are affected by a similar topography to Cape Denison. When the station there was destroyed in a fire in the early 1950s the small field team already at Île des Petrels wintered there instead. Eventually the base was rebuilt on Île des Petrels, and re-named Dumont D'Urville Base in honour of his crewmembers who landed there in 1840.

Our only chart of the area was an ancient French one, complete with pencilled warnings of recifs (reefs) and the odd tentative rock labelled P.A. (Position Approximate). Of more concern to us was the lack of soundings. Much of the chart was simply blank paper. All we had was a single line of well-spaced soundings from the northwest and a sprinkling around the islands and headland. To make matters worse there was no datum to reference our GPS against, and no effective magnetic field to use a hand-bearing compass.

No wonder we had no record of any other yacht ever anchoring in the place.

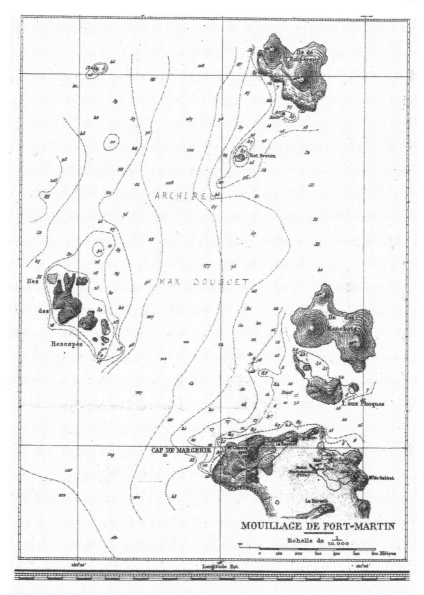

Extract of old French chart No. 6100, showing the Port Martin anchorage

AFTER A CHART BY SERVICE HYDROGRAPHIQUE ET OCÉANOGRAPHIQUE DE LA MARINE

NOT TO BE USED FOR NAVIGATION

2330 HRS

There is a touch of twilit déjà vu this evening as we creep into this fresh anchorage. A biting 20 knot southerly keeps us tucked into the lee of the dodger. We are doing our best to use transits, lining up islets and recognisable landmarks in the same configuration as the marked line of soundings on the

A handful of small empty field huts. They are all that remain of the original French base at Port Martin

chart. In the dimmed daylight the sea is grey and we are watching carefully for any change in the greyness of water around us. Even a swell would be helpful, its swirl betraying rocks lurking below the surface.

The water is deep in the sheltered area between the headland and the adjacent island, except near a reef or close inshore. There is a single shallower sounding on the chart, showing six metres, but the rest appears too deep for a safe scope on our length of chain. To make sure, we make a slow pass right through, watching the sounder and looking for a sign of life around the three small huts perched on the headland. No life and no shallows, so we turn back and locate the underwater shoal.

It is one of those anchorages where the boat seems precarious. Firstly we have no way of knowing if the anchor is simply lying on top of a smooth rock surface. Secondly there is a current of about a knot sweeping through the roadstead from the west while a 25 knot sou'easter funnels through against it.

We sit around a while, debating whether to set anchor watches, before agreeing that a GPS alarm will do. But I sleep lightly all night.

DAY TEN: 28 JANUARY
0730 HRS

The breeze has freshened to 30 knots overnight, probably the local katabatic effect twisted to the sou'east by the slot between these islands and the headland. It's been strong enough during the night to stop us swinging with the tide-change, which is probably why the GPS alarm didn't squeak even once. We

I perch on the pulpit, anxiously searching for rocks in the murky waters below

eat our porridge and Ben, to my surprise, announces that he still wants to
go ahead with our plans to explore the passage between Île des Phoques and
Île des Manchots. It seems pretty risky to me in these conditions. But Ben's
confident. There is a single line of soundings through the narrow western
entrance pass, showing three metres of water – probably sounded from a
French dinghy over fifty years ago.

The light proves to be a problem, reflecting off the water as we work
our way through the pass directly towards the sun. I'm not happy, up in
the bow peering down into streamers of weed which brush past the hull
on either side. If the engine falters now heading into a strong wind like
this, we will immediately sheer off to one side onto the rocks. The anchor
is poised to be released in a flash with the slash of a knife. To improve my
angle of visibility I climb up onto the pulpit and clutch the rolled genoa
for support.

We explore the largely uncharted waters of the archipelago at Port Martin

Time stands still for me but the worst is over in less time than it seems. We are motoring into a widening gap, and I can no longer see the bottom. This side of the island reveals itself as a wide bay, a mix of ice and rock littered with Weddell seals. A potential anchorage perhaps, but exposed to the persistent sou'easterlies.

We circumnavigate the island and resist the temptation to re-anchor. We have been asked not to land at this field base, and there is a great sailing breeze, so we push on with the genoa unrolled, retracing our inward GPS track until we are safely offshore.

Before we left, Ben had secured another important document, this one from the French authorities, handed on to us by the Australian ones. It gave us permission to transit through the French Antarctic quadrant and to visit Dumont D'Urville Base. However it expressly requested that we would not land ashore at Port Martin, because of ongoing archaeological work.

There appeared to be no-one currently staying in any of the huts here, but we had no intention of going against this request. Besides, Ben hates to waste a sailing breeze.

1200 HRS
This part of the Antarctic coast gradually angles its way towards the northwest as we sail towards the French base. We will soon be briefly venturing just

outside the Antarctic Circle. As expected, we are steadily running out of wind. After a rollicking broad reach at over six knots for the first hour we find ourselves increasingly wallowing, until Matt and I eventually persuade Ben to fire up the engine. We don't want to arrive after midnight.

We are beginning to hear fragments of conversations in French on the VHF. Ben tries to call the base on the same channel but there is no response. The sun has returned at last, adding a rich blueness to the sea and a glistening to the ice forms. Bergy bits are everywhere and hand-steering essential.

We are sailing around a large obstacle, the Astrolabe Glacier and a large group of grounded icebergs just off its tongue. It rewards us with the visual opportunity Matt has been waiting for. A band of brash, a huge tabular berg, blue skies and overhead sun. Ben doesn't take too much persuading to allow Matt and me to re-inflate the tinker and putter away.

Matt is really getting the bit between his teeth. Like a budding film director he orders me to steer us this way and that, as he juggles sun angles, exposures and shutter speeds. Finally with the stills all done, he turns his attention to the camcorder. Signalling for Ben to retrace his track for a re-run, he orders me to return to his favoured spot. But *Snow Petrel* doesn't return. We watch, flabbergasted, as Ben motorsails steadily away to the west. Matt's face is a picture of frustration. It hasn't been easy to inflate and launch the tinker, gather all the equipment and experiment for the best filming angles. So we wait, convinced that Ben will turn back in the face of our stubbornness. But no. He's stopped now, quarter of a mile away and showing no sign of returning. There's nothing to do but chase after him

Matt's furious. Too furious even to speak. And I'm not happy either. We haul the tinker aboard and pack away the gear. Matt disappears onto the foredeck in silence. This is the most serious tension we've had aboard on the entire voyage.

I give Ben twenty minutes before speaking about it. It's the second time in two days that I've been piggy in the middle, and I'm mindful of my pledge to respect Ben's decisions on this voyage. But I think back to the failed filming opportunities a week ago when we were working through the pack. It was a sensible decision then to press on, but what's the big hurry now? I put Matt's viewpoint to Ben. After all, it's surely in Ben's interest to get a visual record of this unique voyage.

In the twenty minutes of silence, Ben has had time to consider the situation. He's lost that hard set to his jaw and the steely glare. But he's determined to arrive at the base at a reasonable hour, and we've lost time

Snow Petrel looked stunning as she sailed through brash off the Astrolabe Glacier

drifting around already. In his view, Matt has squandered time unnecessarily taking stills instead of getting movie footage.

I see a chance for compromise not far off our port bow. Another sizable berg and some some safe looking brash. What say you motorsail through there and we buzz around you in the tinker with the cameras? It's agreed. Matt comes to life and we get the footage. *Snow Petrel* looks stunning from where I sit.

1730 HRS

We have contact. After hearing French voices for several hours, Ben has finally managed to get through to someone. In reasonably good English we are asked to wait for the base leader to respond. Half an hour later a female voice, pleasant but with authority, comes on. The boys visibly brighten. She sounds quite perplexed at the thought of a small yacht nearby. Ben assures her that we have the necessary permits, and struggles to pronounce the island that we hope to anchor behind. Her English is certainly better than his French. We hear her voice falter a little though when Ben gives our ETA as a conservative 2000 hrs. He adjusts this to 1900 hrs when she informs him that the base operates on UTC plus 10 hours, an hour behind our Tasmanian daylight time.

At first sight, Dumont D'Urville Base seems to be on the mainland, not an island

1810 HRS (DDU TIME)

The buildings of the base are clearly in sight now, mostly high on top of a rocky island. We've pushed our engine speed up a lot since that radio conversation, and the kettle has just boiled for the first body-wash when I call down the hatch for Matt to wait. In the distance an orange boat has emerged and seems to be speeding towards us. The last time I had a French inflatable approaching like this was in less than friendly circumstances just outside the prohibited zone at Moruroa, and I feel myself involuntarily becoming tense. Reason tells me that this approach bears no relation to that armed encounter, but the reality is that none of us really knows what our reception will be. Ben is hoping that we will at least be able to anchor in the lee of the main island and perhaps be given half an hour to look over the base.

It's not an inflatable after all, but a fair sized workboat. The woman and three men on board seem friendly enough, quickly taking up our invitation to come aboard. There's no sign of paperwork or question of credentials. They introduce themselves with their difficult French names, and stream the workboat astern. All four seem totally at home on a sailing boat and delighted to be aboard.

Gradually it becomes clear what is happening. Alain Pottier is the one who knows these waters well, and will guide us to a suitable anchorage.

The French who piloted us in were all sailors in their own right, back at home

Ariane Richasse is the base leader who will be dealing with any formalities in due course. They are all grinning mysteriously, and Ariane mentions the word 'party' on more than one occasion.

It was small wonder that these four were delighted to be aboard a yacht in these circumstances. We were later to learn that they all had significant sailing experience in France, with Ariane and her husband having built a yacht and sailed across the Atlantic. Alain and Jean-Michel had crewed aboard a tops'l schooner for two years and both had yachts still moored in Brittany. And Dominique had a steel yacht back home too.

But despite our papers granting us permission to visit, none of them had been aware of our existence in Antarctic waters until this afternoon.

1830 HRS
As we enter the narrow passage between the giant runway and Île des Petrels, I'm struck with the contrast between the relatively undisturbed side of Antarctica we have so far experienced, and the evidence here of human impact. To our left is a vast grey flattened surface, scattered with an assortment of machinery and containers. To our right is a high island, its skyline broken by the unnatural straight rooflines of several grey structures. Our berth for the night is to be alongside a large steel floating pontoon, and Alain explains how best to place our lines to deflect the floating ice.

Snow Petrel was berthed on the ice-breaker pontoon next to the abandoned runway

Clearly they are anxious to usher us ashore to meet the team, but we desperately need a wash and tidy up. Our hair is greasy and our clothing odorous. But Ariane is insistent. Come now, bring clothes and towels. Oh, and passports too – a mere afterthought.

A jumble of floating ice links this runway to the main island, but we are told it is not safe to cross. Instead we are ushered aboard the workboat for the eighty metre ride to a concrete jetty. From here it's a spectacular walk up a long steel suspended footpath to the main buildings of the base. The three men peel away into a large building while we follow Ariane to her office in an adjacent two storied structure. Ben gives her our documentation to copy and stamp, and she directs us to the showers.

There's something utterly heavenly about the feeling of peeling away my final layer of thermals and stepping into a waterfall of warmth. Of massaging my greasy scalp and feeling the suds streaming down my naked body. The boys have done this more recently than me, aboard *Orion*, but they both look equally appreciative as we regroup outside Ariane's office. She's stamped our passports and is keen to escort us to the main mess-block.

1920 HRS
This moment would have to rate as the most surreal experience of my entire fifty-three years. As Ben enters the second airlock door of the building ahead of me, I am aware of a crescendo of cheering voices which continues as Matt

and I follow him into a dazzle of colour. From the whites and greys which have
largely become our world we are enveloped in a fluorescence of reds, silvers,
greens, blues, yellows … Our right hands are seized and pumped while large
glasses of bright green liquid are thrust into our left ones.

But as if to utterly confuse our already staggering senses, these life-
forms are more alien than human. For me it is as if I have been truly drawn
into the Restaurant at the End of the Universe – as if reality and fiction have
somehow merged. To my right stands Zaphod Beeblebrox, a large silver-clad
figure with four legs, two arms and a pair of near identical shaven heads.
The figure currently pumping my hand has a green vaguely human face and
an enormous grin. Approaching is a bizarre figure in shiny blue and black,
its appearance distorted by the goggles and tubes sprouting from its head.
Another slightly more human form seems to have an enormous silver antenna
sprouting horizontally from his groin.

Somehow it's assumed that I am skipper of this voyage – an excusable
enough misunderstanding – and I take pains to point out that these are *mes
fils*, that Ben is *le capitaine*. Before long there is a welcome speech and I
indicate for Ben to speak. The circumstances are explained and the party
moves into top gear.

Everywhere there is laughter and good will. The green liquid burns
its way down my throat as another is thrust into my hand and I'm led to a
table covered with green and red pizzas. This is a party to end all parties. I
notice the windows are darkened and the room is lightened by electric ceiling
lights. I become immersed in conversations with a succession of French
accents, some emanating from intergalactic life-forms, and others from more
distinctly human faces.

There is, rather to my surprise, no significant language barrier here.
True the conversations falter a little as we struggle with unfamiliar inflexions
or awkward phrases. I try a little of my schoolboy French and am embarrassed
by how much more competent these people here are with my language than
vice versa.

It becomes slowly apparent that here, just as in any community, there
are the introverts and the extroverts. The introverts haven't dressed up for
the fortnightly Saturday night party (this week themed extra-terrestrial), and
sit embarrassedly in the shadowed corners shaking their heads at the more
brazen antics of their colleagues. I latch on to a serious-looking scientist of
about my age and we engage in conversation about his work on the earth's
magnetic field. Out of the corner of an eye I see Ben and Matt dancing with an
orange-haired alien in a flimsy silver-foil miniskirt.

We were met by a fluorescence of colour and good cheer, like a scene from the Restaurant at the End of the Universe

The music is loud, and interspersed among unfamiliar French lyrics – often to familiar tunes – we regularly hear familiar English music, included for our benefit I suspect. At some point in the evening Zaphod Beeblebrox is laid out for his operation. With the aid of a meat cleaver and appropriate blood-soaked rags he emerges as two separate silver-clad aliens.

0000 HRS

We return to our tiny cold boat in a state of euphoria. We have been promised a guided tour of the Snow petrel colony in the morning, much to Ben's delight. His single regret at our hasty departure from Cape Denison had been the axing of plans to view these birds in their nesting areas. Sleep comes easily tonight.

DAY ELEVEN: 29 JANUARY
1000 HRS

Sunday is a day off at the base. Some duties continue where necessary for continuity of data collection, but the timing of our arrival has been ideal.

An earnest young ornithologist, Samuel Blanc, takes us around the rock slopes of Île des Petrels seeking out the patches of blue spray paint which locate each nesting site. With him is Auregan, a new girl on the base who has been appointed our interpreter. Samuel doesn't need much interpreting though, once he has dredged up his half-forgotten English skills. We find ourselves modifying our own mode of speech and before long we are all chatting like old friends.

What a thrill it is to see these beautiful snow-white birds close up. They have a purity of form and colour, even to their glossy black beak and eyes. Ben's eyes glow with pride and satisfaction. He originally chose this species as a symbolic life form, an ice bird to encapsulate his ambitions. Now he is seeing his selection vindicated beyond his dreams.

But Samuel warns us that despite its innocent and vulnerable appearance the Snow petrel has a powerful defence against predators. It is capable of spitting an acidic saliva for nearly two metres in defence of its nest. For a predatory skua this can result in the loss of its feather waterproofing and ultimately its own life.

We continue past nests of cape petrels and even Wilson's storm petrels, picking our way carefully across the boulders. Samuel warns us to keep an arm raised above our heads as we make our way past screaming wheeling skuas.

Our first close-up view of a snow petrel. Such a beautiful creature—Ben was
enraptured

That way, he explains, they will attack your glove and not your head. Matt
looks ludicrous trying to take photos with one arm raised like a schoolboy
with a question for the teacher.

*Dumont D'Urville Base received much negative publicity during the
eighties when the runway development was approved by the French
government. The rationale was presumably related to mineral exploitation
of the continent, which was dominating international attention in those
pre-treaty days. Building the runway entailed the levelling of three small
islands – all colonised by birds – and reclaiming the sea between them.
It was a huge and controversial project, one seized upon by Greenpeace
which sent a protest vessel to draw attention to the resulting environmental
impact.*

*As white elephants go, this has to rate among the mammoths. Not a
single plane ever landed on the monstrous strip, and everyone I spoke to was
adamant that none ever would. The reasons which I was given were various.
The most plausible related to subsidence issues, and I was shown sections of
the runway which had slumped and a flank which had been eroded away by the
sea. In addition I was told that the logistics of finding an affordable air base
in Australia were too expensive, particularly in view of reduced government
funding. There was clearly a contrast with the huge-scale US programme*

which operates regular flights out of Christchurch in New Zealand. The third reason, often given to me with a gesture of satisfaction, was that the French programme was now preoccupied with environmental concerns and that the impact of large aircraft disturbing the rare giant petrels and fulmars would be unacceptable.

1115 HRS

We have two pressing visits to make before lunch. Auregan shyly escorts us to the post office – a small building sharing all the communications. We recognise Serge immediately as one of last night's extroverts. This morning he is less outrageous as we browse through all the post cards. Of course we have only Australian dollars, but no problem, the conversion from euros is done in a trice. Serge speaks good English, and steadily fills us in on aspects of his job, which encompass much more than just post-master. He shows us into the radio room, the other end of our first tentative contact with this base only yesterday afternoon. The communication stops there unfortunately as, despite his obvious friendlines, the crew-cutted young radio operator has as little English as we have French.

Then we are off for a particularly important stop. 'Le meteo', Auregan calls it, which is an easy enough French word for us to remember and adopt. The meteorologist on duty today is Gilbert, and we recognise his cheerful face well, although this morning it is no longer blue-red-black. We struggle with his name at first – 'zheel-bear' – until he spells it for us and we grasp the transliteration. At his fingertips is a bank of computers and faxes, and in excellent English he outlines an unwelcome prognosis. Two deep Lows are rolling in from the west, bringing several days of gale force winds. Meanwhile the ice is still packed to our north. It looks as if our short stop may become rather more stretched than we expected.

We swing past Ariane's office where Ben has a proposal to offer. Before we have had the chance to say more than our thanks for the overwhelming hospitality, Ariane speaks. She has already spoken to *le meteo* and is well aware of our position. We are invited to join the team for lunch at 1200 hrs, and we are to consider ourselves guests of the base for as long as the weather dictates. We are free to visit any part of the island during this time except the sensitive breeding sites – zones signposted as *acces interdit* and shaded on a map she hands us. We've noticed the fulmar zone already, to one side of the walkway up from the jetty.

To think that only 24 hours ago we were so apprehensive about our reception here! Ben finally gets the chance to put his proposal. Today is

Sunday, as well as being fine weather. He would like Ariane to announce at lunch that *Snow Petrel* will be an open boat this afternoon. And he would like Ariane and a small group of proficient sailors to come for a late afternoon sail. It is one small way we can reciprocate for the great reception we have been given.

By Antarctic standards DDU Base was not a huge one. Compared with McMurdo's 3000-odd American summer party, the French 56 member summer party here was small enough to knit as a team. It would be halving in winter, encompassing only the essential programmes and maintenance staff.

We were struck with the number of relatively young scientists here. The reason lay in the nature of the operation and its limited budget. Back in France the logistical nerve centre, Institut Polaire (also known as IPEV – Institute Paul Emile Victor after its founder), was based in Brittany and dealt with the physical day-to-day aspects of supply and maintenance. The scientific programmes were the responsibility of various French universities, and the majority of the personnel to carry them out were selected from a pool of graduate applicants in their twenties. These young volunteers received a small weekly pay, rather in the nature of a student allowance. Their recompense was not financially driven. On their return they would have the honour of being among a select few, and their chances of acceptance into work of their chosen field would be lifted tenfold.

1200 HRS
The midday meal is a relatively formal affair, with everyone arriving more or less on time and seated randomly at the various tables where food is distributed from trolleys. I am invited to sit with Ariane and a distinguished man of my age who is introduced as Didier Belleoud. He is the previous base leader who has just handed the responsibility to Ariane and is staying for a brief overlap. I learn that both are doctors, and that the policy is for a medically qualified person to be appointed as leader. Ariane is the first female leader at DDU. Didier speaks very passable English and the conversation moves along predictable lines – in this case to our children. His daughter is a journalist covering the America's Cup build-up in Spain, and he is excited to learn that another of my sons, Sam, has been bow-man for the Oracle boss, Larry Ellis, on several major US races.

We are intrigued to see that along with the snail pie on each table is a cardboard cask of Australian wine for general midday consumption. It seems a bizarre combination.

We were delighted to see the New Zealand flag flying proudly alongside the
French tricolour

One important afterthought needed rectifying before we were to put Snow
Petrel *on show. It related to flag etiquette – symbolic but still seen as
important, even in this remote location. Matt had been ecstatic to see the
New Zealand flag flying alongside the French tricolour and IPEV house flag
when we arrived with our passports. It had been a niggle for him on this trip
that* Snow Petrel*'s enormous Australian flag far outsized his tiny Kiwi one
despite our family origins. By rights of course we were sailing an officially
registered Australian vessel, and Ben had correctly used his Australian
passport to clear customs. But having us now symbolically recognised as New
Zealand adventurers gave Matt something to crow about. After all, our two
Kiwi passports outnumbered Ben's.*

*Now that we were in foreign territory it was etiquette for us to fly a
French courtesy flag at our spreaders, something that was overlooked in the
overdrive stage of our preparations. Ariane was happy to lend us one, and
by the time the first guests arrived for a look aboard Ben's little red yacht the
correct flag combinations were fluttering in the freezing afternoon breeze.*

1500 HRS

It's amusing to watch the faces of our small groups of visitors as they are ferried
across for a look aboard. A look of bemusement is almost universal, possibly
at the tiny living area aboard but more likely at the lack of sophistication

Matt floated past in his survival suit like a pink pig

Samuel and Auregan visit SnowPetrel on our open afternoon

in this basic home-built yacht. For most of them, *L'Astrolabe*, the French
icebreaker which brought them south and which is the usual occupant of this
pontoon, was tiny enough.

There is a survival suit training drill happening at the jetty, and Matt
decides to trial Ben's suit for a diversion. So while Ben and I are showing the
visitors around, Matt swims slowly past on his back like a giant pink pig, his
face strangely contorted by the tightness of the hood squeezing his cheeks and
forehead.

We take the base sailors for a sail among the grounded icebergs

Finally we are ready for our sail, and four suitably dressed sailors – the same competent group who met us at sea yesterday – step lightly aboard. The sou'easterly is already freshening and we've taken the precaution of slabbing a reef in the main before they arrived. Alain Pottier has an unpublished chartlet of the local area, and directs us westward around some spectacular grounded icebergs. Even with the soundings on his paper, there is still the chance of a sub-sea pinnacle, so he is piloting us cautiously. They all take turns on the tiller and seem delighted at this unprecedented opportunity to sail among ice.

Matt has stayed back to film us from the top of the island. The breeze sharpens a notch in both strength and bite during the beat back to the pontoon, but the warmth of our fellow sailors' enthusiasm more than compensates for the increased chill factor.

2200 HRS

It has been a successful day and we are exhausted. We have gracefully declined the offer to eat at the base tonight, and Ben is now talking to Mike for the evening sched.

Mike confirms what Gilbert has predicted, and as if to emphasise their predictions we feel *Snow Petrel* heel and shudder in a gust from the sou'east.

Barbara is in Melbourne now and I give in to the temptation of an expensive sat-phone conversation. She tells me, laughing, how she and her brother Red have managed to rig an aerial up on a ladder lashed to the chimney of his suburban house. This way she can still listen to our radio scheds using our portable marine transistor radio receiver.

She's in Melbourne to see our third son Josh off on a fast voyage around Cape Horn on the radical race yacht *Hugo Boss*. It's a black monster of a boat with a swing keel and a million dollar pivoting mast, and is capable of speeds exceeding 35 knots. Sailing with a skeleton crew of five, it's going to be an interesting blast for Josh – he enjoys these sorts of rides. Today Barbara's been out for a tuning run aboard the boat and she's still buzzing. But she's heard Mike's weather and her excitement is tinged with apprehension.

In a few days there are going to be not three but four of her family at the mercy of the Southern Ocean.

Our son Josh has made sailing his career. As a sail consultant for North's he now has his fun on a salary. But he started out the hard way, with two Sydney-Hobarts by 18 years of age, both including the passage to and from Wellington. Since then he's gone on to do most of the big ocean races and not on the slow boats – Capetown to Rio (and back) at 19, Trans Pac, Trans Atlantic (breaking the old mono record), even winning the Fastnet Double. His list of major races overflows two large pages. But, being parents, we best remember him as a ten year old, messing about in Optimists and sailing by the wind on his cheek.

DAY TWELVE: 30 JANUARY
1000 HRS

The wind is a steady 35 knots and after yesterday's balmy afternoon, the air has a vicious bite to remind us that we are still definitely in Antarctica. Getting ashore in the tinker involves a strategy for safety reasons. We hug the immediate shoreline until we are nearly at the ice bridge, then turn and swiftly motor to the jetty. At least this way if the little outboard dies on us we have a chance of rowing to the main island. Ben has the waterproof VHF tucked into his coat pocket as a potential extra cry for help.

Ashore for the day we make our way straight to *le Meteo*. I'm sure we're going to wear a beaten path this way over the coming days. In the cosy warmth of the office Gilbert introduces us to his fellow meteorologists, Patrick and Joseph. This morning Gilbert has been trying to download some ice reports for us, but the cloud has been obscuring the satellites. He shows us the pictures, identifying the subtle shades of white which differentiate cloud from ice. He also shows the barometer graph which accentuates how quickly the pressure is dropping. We'll be here a while, it's obvious.

Before we leave, Gilbert has two more things to show us. One is a framed wind-speed recording, an astonishing 384 km/hr wind gust. We struggle to mentally convert this to knots. A world record anemometer reading, he tells us proudly, before ushering us to his computer screen to show pictures of his dive boat back in France.

With everyone busy at their jobs, the washing machines are free and we take the opportunity to run the smelliest of our garments through. It certainly beats using a bucket and handwringing them to freeze dry.

We spend the rest of the morning in various labs. It's fascinating to learn of the extent of research being carried out. Every tentative knock becomes a welcome. It continues into the conversations around the lunch table, where I learn among many other things that this year's Adélie penguin count on this island alone is up from 11000 to 14000. There is pride in the conservation ethos now beginning to dominate activities at this base, almost as if this new generation wishes to correct the oversights of the previous one. I suspect it is an ethos found elsewhere in Antarctica. I've heard of the huge clean-up operation beginning at the old Wilkes base near Casey for example, the scene of rusting fuel barrels and abandoned machinery acting as a blot on the authorities that allowed it to reach this condition.

During the afternoon we diverge, with Ben heading back to *Snow Petrel* while Matt and I continue to move around. I spend more time down at the marine operations shed with Alain Pottier, the man in charge. He has the straightforwardness of a man who has spent much of his life at sea, and with both our interests in traditional rigs we have a lot in common.

It is a chance to find out more about the dive operations too, a research field which I have already heard something about during lunch. The team of four in this study are embarking on a three-summer study of a unique local species of scallop which is very slow growing and long-lived. The programme has been initiated by an unruly haired and dynamic looking professor, Yves-Marie, who enlisted one of his students, Joelle, as a diver along with two other highly experienced divers, Laurent and Erwan. All three divers seem to be treated with considerable respect around the base and I can understand why. Diving in sub-zero waters is fraught with dangers, and there are many precautions to be observed.

The findings are not just for academic interest. They will be compared with scallop shells in three other locations globally to yield information on environmental change. Back at the lab I'm shown a shell under the microscope.

It's astonishing to see how its layers vary in size, like tree rings, betraying seasonal variations during its five decades of growth. This shellfish may have already been a tiny spat when I was born.

The afternoon passes quickly and is completed with an invitation – nay, expectation – that we join the team for dinner. The moan of wind and flurries of snow outside have done nothing to dampen the free flow of conversation and wine.

Certainly our trip back to *Snow Petrel* is in stark contrast to the warmth and conviviality we have just left. And our freshly filled water-tanks are already beginning to freeze solid.

DAY THIRTEEN: 31 JANUARY
0930 HRS

The decks are caked with snow, and spray lifts off the water in each gust as we accept a ride in Alain's big workboat back to his jetty. We've been asked by Ariane to coordinate with Alain rather than risk our vulnerable tinker when the wind is this strong. I'm looking forward to the chance of thawing out ashore. *Snow Petrel* is like a freezer.

This morning we have decided to visit the atmospheric analysis lab together. This is where Auregan spends her day and I notice that Ben has spruced himself up with a little extra effort this morning. She speaks so well and we are able to have our questions understood and answered without the hesitations we have had in some labs. She and another shy young scientist will be working in this lab through the coming winter as technicians, filtering out ions and particulates from the polar air for global pollution analysis. Eventually, as the conversation strays onto unrelated tangents, we tear ourselves away to leave them to their interrupted routines. I move off to take up an offer from Jacques, the base magnetician.

I have several reasons for this next visit. He and I became friends early in Saturday's party, and I've had several conversations since. He first spent time at this base three decades ago, back when the magnetograph was still the old brass one and when his ship steamed down on dead-reckoning, reaching the ice-cliffs over forty miles off course. He shows me through the small building which houses the new computer-driven analytical equipment. This constantly changing data is regularly transmitted to a nerve centre in Japan where it can be correlated with other information and posted on the web. And why? So that people like me can correct our compass readings for the ever changing location of the magnetic poles.

For contrast he takes me to the old magnetograph house, a non-ferrous structure like Mawson's, containing a comparable vintage brass instrument. It's interesting to reflect on the role this very instrument would have played in determining the compass rose on the charts I used in my boyhood days.

However Jacques is intrigued to hear my mariner's slant on his occupation. Being so tied up with the technicalities, he has never seen a chart which locates the pole and the lines of magnetic variation which radiate out from it like giant curved spokes. Before lunch I hitch a ride with him in Alain's workboat to show him *Snow Petrel*'s Southern Ocean chart. It's good to be able to reciprocate somehow.

And speaking of reciprocating, my conscience, like Ben's, is bothering me. Here we are being treated like honoured guests while everyone works. I find Ariane in her office and ask what tasks might be available for me to make myself useful. She understands my position and allows my name to be added to the meals roster. She will talk to Didier about other opportunities.

The whole business of the magnetic poles is surprisingly complex. Before this trip I understood that the magnetic poles resulted from two magnetic lodes very slowly moving with the convection currents under the earth's crust. Now, after more reading and various conversations with Don, Jacques and Ben, I can see that it is even more complex. Don told us that the South Magnetic Pole moves at speed, up to 30 knots, in a series of loops.

Then Jacques put an even bigger spanner in the works. From his highly technical viewpoint he told me that there is no single South Magnetic Pole. There are several, spread over an area of several square kilometres . He was startled at my request for a specific location for us to visit. However he set to work over the next days to pinpoint a credible current centre of the magnetic field, using the bearing and declination from his instruments. That was to be as good as anyone could hope for.

1200 HRS

Ben has the same sense of obligation when we talk during lunch. He has noticed on the whiteboard that there is to be a short talk after dinner tonight by one of the scientific teams, so he has a word with Ariane who adds a second talk to the board, something about *le voyage de Snow Petrel, illustré.*

Ben and Matt both disappear back to the boat after lunch to blitz the mammoth task of crudely editing Matt's footage and putting together a powerpoint presentation. Meanwhile I've struck up a conversation with another Alain, one of the maintenance staff. As a French Canadian, he is fluently bilingual, and takes me around the workshops. The oldest person on the base, also named Alain, works here as a carpenter. In contrast he has no English whatsoever so we have a very amusing conversation in my schoolboy French, and a good laugh.

Like many Kiwis, I had nursed a long-standing grudge against the French. Their atmospheric nuclear tests at Moruroa had resulted in measurable doses of radioactive isotypes in New Zealand's pastures and milk. My sister-in-law had suffered thyroid cancer possibly as a result of this. And then there was the Rainbow Warrior *sinking in Auckland at the hands of French military divers.*

When Jacques Chirac announced a resumption of underground nuclear tests in the Pacific in 1995, Barbara and I were so incensed that we sailed there as part of a New Zealand protest flotilla – a predictable move after years of protesting against nuclear warships visiting New Zealand ports.

And yet I have never been able to overlook the French achievements in the sailing world. Sailors like Moitessier, Tabarly, and a whole generation of round the world French solo and multi-hull sailors have raced alongside New Zealanders, and deserve recognition for their achievements.

I can understand how a generation of returned soldiers can nurse a hatred for an entire nation, while its children befriend the next generation. Time heals. Attitudes change. This visit was giving me the chance to reflect upon my own prejudices. Should individuals be blamed for the actions of governments? Should the French scientists who rallied against Chirac's tests be tarred with the same brush? Should this generation of young volunteers at DDU be spurned because of an airstrip sanctioned by a bureaucratic regime before they were born?

And as for me, was I blameless? Migrating to an Australia whose government embraced the heartless incarceration of innocent refugees, and leapt willingly enough into a misguided attack on Iraq.

It is people who matter most. Especially in this remote location. In the space of a few days here, my prejudices had simply dissolved.

2030 HRS

For such a short preparation, Ben's and Matt's presentation is going brilliantly. I had been wondering if they'd have an audience at all, when so many people disappeared after dinner. But now the big room is overflowing, and it seems that the entire base may be in here. Ben has asked Auregan to interpret for him

which she does shyly, summarising the key points in the knowledge that much
is self-explanatory. A laugh goes up when Ben screens the state of *Snow Petrel*'s
interior only days before departure. And questions flow as shots of Mawson's
hut appear on the screen. I am surprised at the interest in Port Martin too, until
I realise that despite being a field base, very few people here will have visited it.

It is clear that we have struck a chord here. I can feel the empathy
flowing as they relate to the achievement of doing something so unusual
without many resources or any financial backing. And they like the fact that
Ben is skipper too. I hear a collective intake of breath as some of the heavy
weather sequences are screened, no doubt invoking memories of unpleasant
experiences on their own voyages south.

Ben concludes with heartfelt thanks for our warm reception, and there
are some questions. After a struggle, I give in to my impulse to join him in
closure. It is something I feel I have to do. In speaking, I reflect in as simple a
language as possible, my initial reservations about visiting the French base. And
why. I feel the tension, and suddenly wonder whether these things should have
been left unsaid. But no, I'm committed now, so I spell out how the openness
and warmth of everyone here has, for me, undone decades of prejudice against
an entire nation; how the human side of their country has been revealed.

The tension dissipates. It has been said. And understood.

DAY FOURTEEN: 1 FEBRUARY
0900 HRS

We are cold and tired in our little frozen steel capsule. It was a broken night,
with several large chunks of ice fetching up against the pontoon and turning
it into a noisy giant steel drum. At least this morning is not too windy, though
we are expecting a severe gale tonight.

I hear the work boat arriving and get my gear on. I've arranged to
spend much of the day working with Didier and a few of the maintenance
guys on a big recycling job. I greet them and we walk together to a group of
containers towards the western end of the runway. This part of the base has
such an industrial feel about it that it's hard to imagine I'm even in Antarctica.
That's until we try decanting the big rusty oil drums. Under the waste oil is a
residue of frozen water, and once again the difficulties of working in sub-zero
conditions becomes obvious.

I get the fun job of emptying and crushing several boxes of corroded
beer and coke cans. Somehow the carbonated liquid hasn't frozen solid
when I put the ice pick into them. So my wet weather jacket gets a good

soaking before it freezes up. We spend the morning separating old plastic from metal, debating whether plastic coated wire should be with the non-ferrous metals. It's good to be busy and part of a useful team. And to be accepted. Somehow my words last night have cemented an even better mutual understanding.

As we work, Lilian, the hardbitten helicopter pilot, flies in several net-loads of additional rubbish for us to sort. I'm interested to see his flight path skirting well wide of the fragile fulmer nesting site.

We break for lunch. The wind is picking up now and I have time to change and wash. Didier tells me that will be enough for today. It's too hard to work in a gale.

In its fifty-odd years of operation the base had accumulated a mountain of redundant equipment and debris. (Too recently though to be classified as artefacts by overzealous archaeologists.) Now there was a move to rationalise and remove as much as was practical. Naturally the day-to-day refuse was being been shipped out on a seasonal basis.

Because L'Astrolabe operated out of Hobart, the refuse was destined for a nearby rubbish dump. However Tasmania, having embraced recycling, would no longer accept any containers of unsorted recyclable material. Even the daily kitchen garbage was now being sorted. The expensive alternative would be to ship it back to France. That is why even Didier, former base leader, was busying himself with the unpleasant task of rubbish removal.

1200 HRS

The boys are already ashore and I see them at another table. The meal times are an important focal point. They are also a chance to get special notices across. Today there is a severe lecture from one of the senior maintenance staff. I struggle to pick up a little of his rapid speech. Afterwards Sam Blanc translates for me. With 56 personnel on the base, the water-supply is taking a hammering. All water here is distilled, not just desalinated. The new recruits have been too liberal with their consumption, so to allow the tanks to recover, the washing machines will be temporarily shut down.

Somewhere at this point the divers walk in, half way through the meal. There's a ritual here for strict meal times. The alternative would make kitchen routines difficult. However the divers appear to have special status around here. Two of them join my table, clearly agitated. Erwan has a bandage on his hand and Laurent helps him explain the morning's excitement. From his scallop-collecting work on the seabottom, he sensed a shadow close above him. Looking up he saw the spine-chilling shape of a large Leopard seal. Luckily decompression was not a significant issue for him after such a short time down at this shallow depth, so he escaped with only a graze and a solid dose of adrenaline. But this arrival of a Leopard seal in their waters is going to give them an extra headache over the coming days.

After lunch we tread the walkway back to *le meteo*. The anemometer is recording 85 km/hr gusts already (metric here – knots are unheard of) and predicted to rise tonight. Gilbert is still struggling to gain us a comprehensive satellite ice picture, and hands us one depicting a giant cloud spiral, with a number of hand-drawn red patches and question-marks. It seems there is a very large berg out there with ice dammed up to the east of it. He tentatively suggests that Friday might give us a short weather window, perhaps sailing northwest around the big berg. But today's only Wednesday, and we've got a storm tonight to sit through. Looking out his window we see a horizon of unbroken ice.

It's empty back in the main building, and gloriously warm. The library is full of fascinating French books, and for a while I struggle to follow the photograph captions while the boys try their hand at the pool table. I've got another lab to visit, the fish lab at the other end of the bird lab.

I've spoken to the younger scientist in here already, and we've seen some of the footage he's collected using a remote undersea camera. When I quiz him on his excellent English and slight Australian accent, he explains that he was an exchange student in Bunbury, south of Perth. The slide show he has for me on his laptop is full of vibrant colours and exotic shapes. His specialty is invertebrates, and he tells me that these icy nutrient-rich waters yield a far greater biomass of invertebrate life than temperate waters.

He has a particularly exciting discovery to reveal, something that all biologists dream of, I'm sure. It's a new discovery, a species of sea cucumber with a shell. I suggest that he might name it after himself but he emphasises that such practice is not acceptable in modern science. However he can take the credit for its discovery, which is good enough for him.

1500 HRS

I gather the boys for another slide show invitation, this time with Katelle, the base photographer. Her boyfriend Lilian, the helicopter pilot, isn't flying in this gale, but his English isn't good so he leaves the talking to her. She was involved in the filming of 'The March of the Penguins' here at DDU last year, and tells us about it. But the pictures she wants to show us today were taken when she was a driver on a recent *raid* – transit – between this base and Concordia, the joint Italian-French base several thousand kilometres inland.

Her photos show a convoy of tracked vehicles, led by a snowplough, each towing multiple giant sledges across a vast white featureless plain. One shot shows them all drawn up in a huge circle, like covered wagons in the pioneer West, banked with drifts of snow to the top of the cabs. During these extreme blizzards a generator runs constantly, heating the vehicle engines to prevent them seizing irrevocably. It's a fascinating insight into another facet of Antarctica, and we linger with a dozen questions.

We had noticed, early in our visit, a small cluster of buildings several kilometres away on the continental coast-line. This was Cap Prud'Homme, a small transit station for preparing cargo. It also received any passengers flying in from Concordia or McMurdo on a small twin engined Otter, landing on an ice strip a little way up the slopes. It was connected to DDU mainly by helicopter, but early in the season heavy goods could be transported there across the sea ice.

'Le Raid' was the name given to the supply convoy which set off several times a season for the ten day haul up to Concordia. From a logistical viewpoint, le Raid was also a base, a mobile one with its own portable accommodation block and supplies. It had to be fully self-sufficient, travelling a GPS route in such a demanding environment.

Concordia itself was a cylindrical structure, several stories high with its footings simply drilled into the slow moving ice cap. Its location took advantage of the virtually pristine atmosphere for atmospheric sampling and analysis. In addition, the clarity of air made it an excellent observatory.

1930 HRS

All three of us are a little anxious tonight about getting back to the boat, but we have been told that the Wednesday night movie, shortly to be screened, will be 'MASH', in English with French subtitles in our honour. So we will be staying late. But Ben has a sched to keep, and slips away for a ride with Alain, hoping to return. He has arranged to talk to a mate, Scott Lachlan, who is captain of *Aurora Australis*, the Australian icebreaker. Before the movie begins screening we have a radio message from him to say that he won't make it back.

The movie is amusing, but completely out of place in this environment. It's nice to have the black-out screens up again and experience the illusion of night-time. But outside we can hear the shriek and growl of a storm-force blizzard, and I wonder how we will get back tonight.

Ariane has anticipated this though. There's no way she will allow us or Alain to risk a boat in these conditions. Instead she has already arranged for Joelle to move into Stephanie's room tonight so that Matt and I can sleep in the

The short distance from pontoon to the jetty on the main island would quickly become unsafe to cross in a strong gale

bunks in her vacated room. It's a sensible and thoughtful gesture, though I feel embarrassed to have allowed the situation to develop this way.

Nevertheless, both Matt and I are gaining yet another fresh experience tonight, our only night actually ashore in Antarctica. In my bunk the heated air is stifling, while up here on the second floor I can feel the entire building shudder in the violent gusts. Sleep doesn't come easily.

DAY FIFTEEN: 2 FEBRUARY
0930 HRS

We've washed and eaten, and the blizzard is still buffeting the complex. I manage to raise Ben on the VHF and it's clear that we won't be able to see one another until much later. I've got my day mapped out though. I'm on the meals roster today, and I've landed a job helping Didier and Ariane do a stock-take of the souvenir items in the base shop. It's a good chance to practise counting in French again and time passes quickly. Apart from the stifling heat in this block, I'm enjoying myself.

1130 HRS

My partner on the meal roster today is Serge, the communications boss. He's a fun guy and seems pretty relaxed about our duties. We eat half an hour before the others, and make sure that the tables are set well beforehand. I'm amused to be decanting Aussie cask wine into French wine bottles. It's something that live-aboard yachtees like us do all the time, but I hadn't expected to be doing it down here – or even to see wine on the table in the middle of a work day either.

After being nervous about this job, I'm soon enjoying myself, passing big plates of rabbit stew onto the tables and using my limited repertoire of French phrases while I collect plates and replenish the tables. I'm actually beginning to feel part of the furniture around here in a comfortable way. It still seems strange, though, to be involved in an experience like this without Barbara around. Having been entwined in a married relationship since the age of 19, it sometimes is hard to separate myself as an individual.

After lunch there are dishes to clear away. I'd envisaged myself toiling at the sinks for an hour or more, but a dishwasher is taking care of that so Serge and I are free to go.

1600 HRS

At last Ben is ashore. The wind has eased below gale-force now though there's still the occasional snow flurry. Ben tells us that he had an interesting talk to *Aurora Australis* in a long sat-phone call last night. Scott is over two thousand miles to our west, but he had some good tips to help us get out, and his ice-information looked hopeful.

Together we trek to *le meteo*, where Gilbert and Patrick both agree that things look good for tomorrow. There's another nasty low moving this way, but if we get away in the morning we should have 36 hours to get ourselves clear of the pack before the next gale. Charming!

The next stop is Ariane's office. Ben has an invitation for her to visit *Snow Petrel* this evening after dinner and bring her slideshow of a recent sailing trip to South Georgia. But also we need to let her know our departure prospects.

Ariane has another meeting in mind. This one is with Patrice, the longstanding logistical director for IPEV, a man of enormous standing around the base. He and Ariane have clearly talked beforehand and he quizzes us on the status of our provisioning – fuel in particular. They both have the impression that we may be low on diesel and water, and could need assistance. Ben's response is adamant. We are fully self-sufficient and have ample supplies for our return. 'Are you not happy with our hospitality?' asks Patrice unexpectedly, and we all reassure him that we have been overwhelmed by the generosity we have received. But Ben takes pains to explain how we perceive the difference between hospitality and re-provisioning. There is a principle at stake and his point is taken. We shake hands on this understanding.

In recent times there has been a spate of well publicised cases of private expeditions requiring assistance and provisions from various bases. The French base is well off the track but others receive regular requests. Even aircraft fuel has been requested and refused, amid a howl of media indignation.

The general public is largely unaware of the expense and logistical energy involved in freighting carefully calculated quantities of fuel and provisions south to this frozen continent. We were conscious, ourselves, of being a drain on the French resources simply by eating with them, but had been requested to do so in circumstances which involved etiquette and hospitality. It was clear on both sides that we had adequate food of our own but that the mealtimes allowed a mutual exchange of social and intellectual value.

Various bases have established policies to protect them from casual demands for re-supply. Some will give downright refusals. Others will prioritise according to the degree of necessity. And we have heard that the large US bases will supply anyone, but at enormous cost, to compensate the real costs as well as to deter the casual visitor.

A private Spanish sledging party had recently requested French permission to come to DDU on the final leg of a transcontinental expedition. Head office in France had turned down the request, rather to the embarrassment of some of the team here at the base. After threatening to come regardless, the Spaniards eventually altered course to a Russian base further west and a stand-off was averted.

We had no need or desire to be involved in such issues. Patrice and Ariane were genuinely concerned for our safety and we appreciated their offer. But for our own self-esteem we intended to complete our voyage without assistance. Hospitality notwithstanding.

DAY SIXTEEN: 3 FEBRUARY
0900 HRS

There is a dying easterly and plenty of sunshine this morning. We launch the tinker for the trip ashore – to *le Meteo* of course. Gilbert has the perfect gift, an excellent sat-pic of the sea to our north. The clouds have gone and the ice is

Almost the entire base turned out for this shot. The dark figure between Ben and Ariane is a bronze bust of the French polar pioneer Paul Emile Victor

well scattered. Gilbert embarrassingly plies us with more gifts: a book, a large stuffed toy emperor penguin, calendar and postcards. Even some specially tailored weather summaries.

Ben manages to talk on the HF base radio to Xavier, captain of *L'Astrolabe* which is due to arrive at the base tomorrow. The icebreaker will be listening for us, and able to help if an emergency arises.

It's hard to get away. Michel and Nicolas in the kitchen have prepared us a huge food parcel, while Didier and Ariane have wine for us. Real French stuff, not decanted! We are overwhelmed.

We swing by the bird and fish labs, where Samuel has prepared Matt a CD of his photographs. Ben has a small gift for the fish lab, a home-made version of the bait catcher we used when the kids were young. Hugs and handshakes abound before we eventually return to get *Snow Petrel* ready for a midday departure. It's a busy time, deflating and stowing the tinker, finding homes for our gifts and securing various items of loose gear. But at last we are ready to move off the pontoon.

The word has spread, and all along the skyline and even rooftops, we see waving figures. As we pass the western point of the main island, we are startled by a loud blast from a fog-horn, and a green flare hisses skyward while another dazzles from a waving hand. Matt struggles to focus his camcorder as another flare streaks upward. There is waving and the sound of distant voices shouting final farewells as we glide our way out into the clear passage towards open sea.

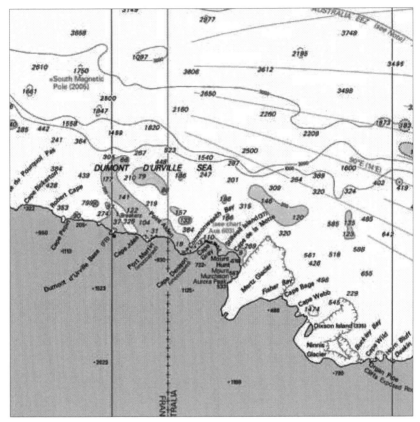

Chart showing the South Magnetic Pole and the French Dumont D'Urville Base

PHASE 8

To the Pole, and Home

One of my all-time favourite books was a childhood one – 'Winter Holiday' by Arthur Ransome. It is one of those classics that survives through generations. A bunch of kids rig their sledges with sails when an English lake freezes over. They even set up home aboard an iced-in houseboat. Being English, their focus is on the North Pole and the houseboat becomes the Arctic exploration vessel, Fram. *And naturally their ultimate goal is to make their way to the elusive North Pole, somewhere at the head of the lake.*

The copy we bought for our own sons has been loved almost to death. It survives with the aid of many careful repairs. Ben even borrowed it to re-read recently. And I often wondered, whenever the boys rigged their makeshift squaresails on the Maid*'s dinghies, how much influence that book had on their own lives.*

DAY SIXTEEN: 3 FEBRUARY
1230 HRS

Once again, we are on our own. Exhilarated, yet somehow subdued. I feel as if we have been given so much for so little in return. But now I can look up to see the French tricolour still fluttering at the spreaders and feel contented, something I would never have felt before this visit.

The wind is ideal for our departure, about 20 knots on our aft quarter. We don't need the mains'l reefs that we slabbed in as a precaution before departing, so we shake out full canvas and set a course of due north.

There is a thick brew of brash ice everywhere now, which we can't avoid sailing through. Instead we ease sheets to slow the impact as we push through the worst patches, the hull ringing like a drum as dozens of pumpkin-sized lumps of ice clank their way along and under the steel plating.

Hand steering for this first leg is essential, *Snow Petrel* weaving a slalom path for the first hours between bergy bits the size of cars.

DAY SEVENTEEN: 4 FEBRUARY
0230 HRS

It's déjà vu yet again. My night watch of course. We're 60 miles offshore by now and at one stage we'd hoped there might be no pack. But we are inside it now. And the twilight is exceedingly dim. There's some visibility, but only for about 100 metres distance. Besides, it's snowing.

On tonight's sched Mike was talking about the slow-moving Low still to our northwest. The computer model he's using predicts that it will rapidly deepen and develop into a bomb. It's the same scenario *le Meteo* and even *Aurora Australis* were predicting. He advised us to slow down and sail westward to let it pass some distance to our north. That strategy suits us anyway because the position that Jacques has given us for the South Magnetic Pole is to our north-west.

But right now my options are closing in. I've been motorsailing northwards through loose pack under full main since I came on watch, but it's rapidly thickening, and I'm beginning to run out of options. I yell to Ben to come up and take the helm so I can dump the main. There's still a light southerly and with the sail up, I'm worried that I won't be able to stop fast enough if I get us jammed into a tight spot somewhere in the murk just ahead.

Ben grabs some warm gear and relieves me briefly; then once we're manoeuvrable again he goes below to dress properly. The exercise was just in time, as we've reached a solid band of impenetrable ice and our best option looks to be eastwards here. It's Saturn's rings all over again, and I'm not particularly happy with the eastern track, but the ice is packed solidly to the west as far as my short visibility span can show.

I see Ben putting the kettle on before he comes up, and I'm pleased to be able to pass the decision-making over once he's on deck. It'll probably be another couple of hours before we get decent light, and even then the visibility won't extend much further unless it stops snowing.

From up the mast, Ben yells and points at a small gap just ahead to our left and I take the engine out of gear to lose way before easing her through. Once that band is behind us, there's another not far ahead but this time Ben signals to go west. That's a relief.

We aren't experiencing the same sense of danger tonight as we did a fortnight ago when we first encountered pack ice. Somehow familiarity has bred a sense of complacency. Back then, aeons ago it seems, we were even skirting for miles around icebergs to avoid brash, yet this afternoon we were ploughing through it under full sail. The human brain is a complex organ, progressively reprogramming itself from an initial cautiousness as it reappraises the safe limits. Back in my brief mountaineering days I experienced this too. Then came a family of young kids and suddenly the caution re-appeared. Most of the guys who were climbing back then are dead now, usually killed pushing personal limits. So the moral is that we mustn't become too complacent tonight.

Steadily we keep pushing west, occasionally squeezing north through a gap in each successive band. I stay up during Ben's watch, occasionally putting out a VHF call to L'Astrolabe in case she's in the vicinity. Our theoretical VHF range is about 20 miles, so the further we push westward, the less likely we are to be within their circle of hearing. It is a comfort though to know that there's a potential source of assistance not far away if something goes dramatically wrong. In an emergency we could contact the base via our big HF radio, and have our position relayed to the ship. But we certainly don't intend to get ourselves into such a serious pickle.

0530 HRS

I'm beginning to sense the ocean breathing again now. The bands have broken into clumps and we are weaving our way through these in a zigzag northerly direction. I put the kettle back on and call Matt, suddenly realising that he'll be wanting more footage. He does, and he's quite cross about not being called up when it was thick. I'm not too sympathetic though – he must have been woken at times by the noise we've been making on deck.

Matt's only just in time. The pack has thinned out into little more than brash and growlers. The sun is poking its head up above the clouded horizon and the GPS shows us to be 73 miles north of land. Ben sets Matt's course direct to Jacques' waypoint, 13 miles to our northwest, and we collapse into our bunks.

0800 HRS

Somewhere through the confused haze in my dreams I hear an insistent voice. And I'm being shaken. The engine is idling. Matt's voice. 'We're there.' It means nothing to me.

'The Pole, Dad!' Ah – I'm sensible again.

Outside we're drifting on a fairly calm sea, heaving with a swell from somewhere to our northwest. The GPS reads 0.01 miles from the waypoint that Ben entered as S-POLE. Thinking of Jacques' 'centre of field', that's close enough for me. I throw the danbuoy overboard and put the kettle on. A cup of tea may clear my fuzzy head.

Matt and I talk about it while Ben sleeps on, unaware. Until now we haven't given much thought to any sort of ceremony. Matt hasn't had a chance to make a cake, or prepare anything special. And even champagne doesn't sound too appealing at this time of day. We know Ben's a bit sceptical about Jacques' waypoint. It's to the southeast of the position marked on our two-year-old chart and we understand the pole tends to gradually drift to the northwest over the years. But I'm of the opinion that Jacques has the instruments for an up-to-date position. And if Don was right about the way the pole moves in loops, then we may be experiencing a southern tangent here. It's the best we can do, acting on good scientific advice, so we have to believe it.

What we decide to do is wait a while and let the light breeze drift us away from the danbuoy pole so that we can experience finding our way to a visible location. In fact it's a good time for me to shut the engine down and top up the gearbox oil. While I'm down there I check things out and tighten the shaft gland as well.

By the time I've finished we've drifted a quarter mile from the waypoint, and it's time to wake Ben. He's bleary eyed and surprisingly unenthusiastic at first. A combination of sleep deprivation and private doubts about the accuracy of this location have clouded his sense of achievement. But it is a rare achievement to be here, I remind everyone, myself included as we motor slowly towards the waypoint. It proves a lot more difficult to find the danbuoy than I expected, as it has drifted a little west of the original position. Matt disappears below and re-emerges with cameras and the little Kiwi flag. He has a triumphant look on his face, as even Ben can see that the enormous Australian flag is too big for the danbuoy pole.

It's a slightly bizarre little impromptu ceremony as I tie the Kiwi flag to the danbuoy and declare the South Magnetic Pole to be a New

With the Kiwi flag flying to announce our brief possession of the South Magnetic Pole, I quickly check that the needle actually does point straight down

Matt proves to Ben that we really are at the South Pole

Zealand possession, while Matt captures the occasion for posterity. Ben is grinning now too, and we all take turns to be photographed holding our simple orienteering compass on its side so that the needle is pointing vertically.

None of us is in a hurry to push on, so we sit in the cockpit with chocolate and a hot drink. It's slowly registering now that we have actually achieved all the improbable goals Ben had set before we left. All except the significant challenge of getting home again of course. We are clear of the pack but remind ourselves that we're not yet clear of ice. While we are still in iceberg waters there will be growlers still lurking among the brash, and we will need to get north of the worst of the ice before the next Low comes through. At the back of all our minds is the threat of an approaching storm, and it is beginning to sink in that between us and home is the entire width of Southern Ocean yet again. Perhaps this time it may not be so kind to us.

There's one thing left to do before I hop into my bunk. The sat-phone is back in its locker, sealed up in a plastic container. I dial Barbara with the good news. It's not every day she gets a phone call from the South Pole, even the magnetic one. She's chuffed of course, but even more chuffed to hear that we're finally north of the pack. Having us trapped behind that barrier has been dominating her thoughts for days now. She has a last word of advice though, and it would be tempting fate to ignore it: 'Don't relax too much yet. There could still be ice around.'

We had looked upon our first Southern Ocean crossing as something akin to running the gauntlet, an old childhood game I used to play in which we would take turns to run quickly between two lines of children who would all be trying to whack us with their belts. The faster we ran, the less a lucky strike would hurt our padded bottoms.

We were already aware of an apparent reduced risk in this southern latitude south of the main track of the Low centres. But recently there had been a succession of these systems tracking very close to the Antarctic coast, and these were a worry. Overall though we were aware of the largest danger of all, the monster greybeard waves of the westerly wind belt. These waves, often exceeding 12 metres in height, are pushed up during periods of persistent westerly gales.

During our trip down we had been relatively lucky to have a succession of wind shifts which interrupted the formation of monster greybeards. And we had been able to time our departure for a period of moderately settled weather. This time we would not be able to time our arrival in the fifties and forties for any significant window. We would have to take whatever the gods threw at us over the coming two or three weeks. Perhaps we'd get leniency for good behaviour.

2100 HRS

We've reset the ship's time back to Tasmanian time, and Ben's talking to Mike on the sched. Mike's talking about Jocelyn Foganolo's article about us in today's Hobart newspaper, the 'Mercury'. He hasn't actually read it, but has been told that it makes us sound like significant adventurers. Another mate, Rob, who lives on his ketch in our marina, breaks in to the radio conversation to confirm this. We laugh about it. We don't feel ourselves to be in the same league as real adventurers. Sure we've taken a few calculated risks, but all has gone well and it's been a great cruise.

DAY EIGHTEEN: 5 FEBRUARY
0500 HRS

It's snowing quite hard and has been blowing a fairly solid easterly all night, up to 35 knots. We've been bucketing along and haven't seen any ice for 24 hours. I'm getting fairly relaxed about the ice watch now, but as we're still so far south, at 63 degrees 45 minutes, I still need to look around fairly regularly. It's hard with the dodger windows and dome drifting up with snow so quickly. Also the visibility is down to only 100 metres.

I pop out of the dodger briefly to wipe the dome and glance around. Would you believe it – right in our path, only ten boat-lengths away, is a big lump the size of a truck! I have just enough time to disengage Sooty and push the tiller hard over. I'm left quite shaken. That one had our name on it. Somewhere in the back of my mind I've been thinking about what Barbara had to say yesterday morning, words that fairly well guaranteed an iceberg in our path. In fact it is probably the fate-tempting nature of her warning that has been keeping me vaguely vigilant.

Even as the bergy bit sweeps past *Snow Petrel*'s flank I feel the breeze easing, and the snow is beginning to thin out. As the horizon reappears I see not one but two big bergs only about a mile to the east, and a line of brash streaming downwind towards us. I'm reminded of the two we saw a full day north of the others during our southbound trip. Perhaps these are their brothers, broken away from some giant parent tabular berg in an outer orbit.

As so often happens, our watchkeeping became readjusted for the voyage home. Somewhere after the long night negotiating the pack, possibly when the ship's clock was reset, the formal roster became transposed. There was no piece of paper pinned up this time. The routine of Matt-Jon-Ben was too firmly ingrained. It simply slid back two hours.

Ben emerges from his cave for a bowl of slops. We found the dog bowls to be very stable plates

For me it meant losing the midnight dogwatch – that became Ben's. For Ben it meant no longer doing scheds during a watch, probably a good thing all round, though we were almost always awake during the scheds and able to cover his lookout duties. Those were the highlights of our days.

2100 HRS

A new sound has developed during the afternoon, one we were expecting. The sound of three timpani randomly clonking in three different low tones under my bunk – a surprisingly melodic noise. The frozen compartments in the watertanks are beginning to thaw out at last, with each diminishing rectangular iceblock surging from side to side as we gently roll.

It's something we had tried to avoid by leaving the refilling until our departure from Cape Denison, but of course the delay at DDU wrecked that clever plan. I don't mind the noise though. Two reasons. The seawater must have warmed to above zero now, and also we can put away the annoying water container that we've been sucking water out of for the past fortnight. That'll mean a bit more space in this cramped little cabin.

I'm quite pleased with myself tonight. I managed to cook up a chile con carne using soy mince, baked beans, chile sauce and red wine – from a cask of course. For a touch of green, we had some of the *Orion* frozen beans which are still in a bucket of ice up in the fo'cs'le. Matt says Barbara will be impressed with my improved culinary skills. But I notice he's commented on my liquid rice in the logbook.

Mike's talking on the radio to Ben about the Low. It has been on our minds ever since we left, and on this afternoon's fax it seemed to be tracking directly towards us. But Mike's telling us now that the prognosis has changed. His model now shows it stalling and splitting in two. It has been a classic false alarm, and all this westing we've been sailing has been largely unnecessary. But we're not complaining. It's an enormous relief to have that worrisome weather-bomb removed from the picture.

As soon as Ben comes off the sched, we harden up the sheets to a course of 315 degrees. We're still sailing towards the north-west, mainly because the wind is still a 15 knot northerly. It was fresher during the day, getting up to 25 knots, but tonight it seems to be easing and veering slightly to the nor'east. Typical! At this stage of our south-bound trip we were headed for three days by southerlies and now we're being headed by northerlies. Such is life.

DAY NINETEEN: 6 FEBRUARY
1600 HRS

It's happy hour and everyone's pretty happy. We even enjoyed a whole can of beer each. Today has seemed like a holiday. Appropriate really, as it's New Zealand's national day today, Waitangi Day. We've been drifting along at between two and three knots all day, close-hauled in a light nor'easterly. Ben took advantage of the upright hull this afternoon and sounded the fuel tank. It seems that we have about 30 hours worth of diesel left, so there's absolutely no point using the engine.

We're comparing our books. Ben's romping through a 1299 page epic called 'London' and I've bagged it next. I'm reading Mawson's 'Home of the Blizzard' and Matt has discovered Hammond Innes at last.

Before dinner, in a fit of enthusiasm I wash my underwear, only to discover that the bucket has a small hole in the bottom. I even manage to repair the galley cupboard door that has needed its hinges fixed since the knockdown.

The sun is shining and despite the fact that we are still south of 62 degrees, we somehow feel as if summer is returning. It's reflected in Ben's cheerful bounce today too. He's offered to cook a fancy meal tonight, coq au vin – chicken in wine – with roast veges, and from where I'm sitting, it smells great.

DAY TWENTY: 7 FEBRUARY
0000 HRS

It's a properly dark night tonight. There's still a faint blueness to the sky but most of the stars are visible now, reflecting off the surface of an oily sea. For most of my watch we have been ghosting along at little more than a knot. And now that it's time to get Ben up I'm reluctant. This is quite magical.

Pfffffffff. It's a familiar noise, startling in its unexpectedness, but joyous in its implications. A friendly visitor alongside us in the darkness. Forgiving its bad breath, I slide towards the starboard rail. Through the gloom I detect a darkness protruding motionless above the water alongside. A large dark shape, a head – not a fin or tail – suspended there. Somewhere is an eye, probably wondering what this alien creature with its giant wing and wallowing underbody is doing in its ocean. I talk to it softly, as is my habit, and it exhales again. Then with a barely discernible swirl it is gone.

I wait a while before calling Ben. These moments are our rewards for perseverance.

Whale sightings had been a significant part of most voyages. But actual visits like this one were a rarer treat. Dolphins would often come of course, homing in on us from miles away to frolic alongside and ride the pressure wave at the bow. Their enthusiasm was always a treat.

Most whales are part of a small pod, so it is reasonable to assume that this one was a lone male, perhaps visiting with courtship in mind. Our most memorable visits have been bulls. One big humpback once scared Sam – alone at the helm – out of his wits by breaching right alongside the Maid *near New Caledonia, showering the entire boat with spray as he crashed back into the water on his belly.*

*Ben and Josh had a less frivolous experience once though, careering at 18 knots into a nearly submerged sperm whale on a mid-Tasman race yacht (*Whispers 2*). It was an abrupt halt, sudden and frightening. Fin keels and rudder skegs are so vulnerable, but in this case it was the poor whale that was worse off. Ben recalls seeing blood in the water but the pandemonium aboard dominated the moment and by the time the damage was assessed there was no sign of any stricken creature. Other yachts have been much less lucky.*

0530 HRS

This is copybook sailing. We are just crossing the 62nd parallel, and the wind has gradually kept veering during the early morning. It is now a southerly, and has freshened to 15 knots. The thermometer is sitting on zero, but I'm used to the cold now and the wind is from behind so it's not in my face.

We've dumped the main and set up the removable forestay with a second headsail boomed out on the opposite side to the genoa. 'Twinning' we call this, a classic tradewinds rig. (Ah to be back in those balmy trades again.) *Snow Petrel* is rolling heavily in the confused swells without any steadying canvas, but it's a small price to pay for the pleasure of forging through the water at over five knots again, direct for Tasmania.

1500 HRS

This afternoon we've decided to watch a movie. It's Ben's idea, as we're definitely clear of ice now, and we're sailing so beautifully in a 20 knot sou'westerly with Sooty steering beautifully. Matt's going to have to jump up regularly to look around in the dome, and of course bring us salted peanuts.

It's a French movie, an old 8 mm one converted to DVD. We were given it by Ariane, who has sailed with Jérôme Poncet, the main character in this documentary. His yacht, *Damien*, is as much a classic for the French as the Hiscocks' *Wanderer* yachts or Robin Knox Johnson's *Suhaili* are to the British. Even though we can't understand much of the dialogue, we have a great time watching *Damien* wandering her old fashioned way around the world, Jerome and his mate largely hand-steering with ropes from inside the dodger. Those albatrosses on the screen may well be the grand-parents or great-aunts of the ones sweeping past *Snow Petrel* now as we lounge on the starboard bunk, laptop lashed to the table.

DAY TWENTY-ONE: 8 FEBRUARY
1300 HRS

The GPS has counted down the 60th parallel, and we've just re-entered the Furious Fifties. I've logged an entry about leaving the sultry sixties but am not going to tempt fate with anything derogatory about the fifties. This belt has my full respect, even though today we have only five knots of breeze and a little watery sunshine. For a few hours earlier we simply dropped all sail and sat, rolling heavily in an oily swell.

Matt has been pestering Ben all morning about inflating the tinker for some footage, but Ben's not keen to dig it out from deep in the starboard quarterberth stowage area. Instead Ben has come up with the simpler option of blowing up the cheap plastic canoe we brought along as an extra. As it slowly expands into a recognisable shape I notice the attached warning

Snow Petrel rolls her gunwales under, becalmed at 60 South ...

... while we take turns to paddle Ben's cheap plastic kayak — not to be used in open sea!

label – NOT FOR USE IN OPEN SEA. Ha! As a precaution we tie a long light floating rope to it and Matt eases himself in with his precious camcorder. It looks precarious but eventually both Ben and I take a turn to paddle around *Snow Petrel* and see her from a dolphin's viewpoint.

The worst part of the exercise is getting in and out. *Snow Petrel* is rolling so heavily without any sail up, that her decks are going under in one moment, and two metres up in the next. It's rather like a liquid see-saw. But we all survive the exercise and Matt has his precious footage.

After finishing our frolic, the weather gods give us our breeze back and we celebrate the day with a special happy hour. Somehow we feel as if we are nearly home now. Even though the hard part is probably still ahead.

DAY TWENTY-TWO: 9 FEBRUARY
1200 HRS

We are back in business today, all powered up in a 30 knot breeze that has gradually been veering toward the west from the south since midnight. It's not pleasant sailing, but certainly satisfying. We can put up with discomfort when we're smoking along in the right direction.

Matt has logged another milestone during the early hours, our first rain in nearly a month. Liquid from the sky, not just snow. We're already at nearly 58 South, and every now and then, a wave picks *Snow Petrel* up by her tail and gives her a big shove forward. Maybe in Josh's language it's not quite surfing – his flying machines will sit on the face of a wave for minutes at a time. But it's great to see the GPS speed surge up to nine knots for a moment, and feel the power as she lifts.

Sooty isn't so happy about this turn of events though. He's been a bit sulky during my watch, and I've had to help him out at times when *Snow Petrel* decides to slew off to port in a semi-broach. To help Sooty out I roll the genoa away entirely and alter course ten degrees to starboard.

Then a movement catches my eye. It's the compass card swinging again. After all this time jammed on south, it's now free again, pointing northwards. Almost enough cause for a celebration.

DAY TWENTY-THREE: 10 FEBRUARY
0600 HRS

It becomes mind-numbing, this crashing to windward. Not dangerous, but jarringly uncomfortable. We've been driving hard into this 30 knot nor'westerly all night, and a dark night it was too. Wet and wild. How Matt managed to cook that bolognaise in those violent conditions I'll never know. We've taken three slabs out of the main and left not much genoa unrolled. The stays'l is working hard now.

I see Ben's head pop up inside the hatch dome. He must have finished pulling down the latest weather fax. I slip it open a crack and call down for his interpretation. Consistent nor'westerlies all day, he thinks. Pretty much as Mike predicted last night. But he's located another small problem this morning. For some unknown reason, the electric bilge pump has become too feeble to keep up with the ingress of water through the aft deck hatch. So we're going to have to add something else to our watch job-description – hand-pumping the deck-mounted bilgepump once an hour until the waves stop sluicing along the leeward side-decks.

Mike Harris is one of those enormously understated characters who crop up occasionally in a lifetime. With his wife, Di, and their now grown-and-flown daughter, he built the steel yacht Pangolin 2 *in England during the eighties and slowly sailed to the Pacific on a 'lame seagull' voyage, stopping for a year or two in each of a variety of locations for the purpose of replenishing coffers.*

His passion is radio communications and marine computer programs. Practical stuff like do-it-yourself compass adjusting, worldwide tides, astronav programs, satellite tracking and HF radio emailing.

Our paths nearly converged on numerous occasions during a decade. He was a radio operator at Moruroa on the New Zealand navy ship Tui *but we didn't meet him there. Nor when both boats were berthed in Auckland only eight miles apart. Not even when we were both in Sydney's Pittwater in 1999. We didn't actually meet until* Pangolin 2 *and the* Maid *relocated to Tasmania and found each other anchored at Bruny Island.*

Mike did not miss a single night of scheds for us during Snow Petrel*'s voyage, plotting us on his 'yotreps' website for all to see. Every night he was there for us, regardless of any inconvenience. Now that is true dedication.*

DAY TWENTY-FOUR: 11 FEBRUARY
0000 HRS

It's dark, drizzling with virtually no wind. I'd far rather have yesterday's discomfort than this frustrating lack of progress.

Ben climbs sleepily up the companionway ladder for the watch change. He agrees with me that this wallowing is not doing the sails any good. Best to drop everything except the stays'l and wait. Sooner or later some wind will happen along. It has to. These are the Furious Fifties.

1100 HRS

It took a while, but we're back in the breeze again. I was the lucky one. Both the boys were reading through their night watches – with the GPS stuck on 738 miles to go – but I got a light westerly during mine, at about 0500 hrs, and managed to get us under way again at four knots.

Now we're all awake for our treat. It's 55 South and we've reached the half way mark. We are 708 miles from DDU with 708 left to Tasmania. And outside, the sea is full of birds again, especially storm petrels. The Convergence. We celebrate with a big plate of bacon and eggs each and then Matt has a field day chasing birds with his zoom lens. It's tricky work from the deck of a heaving yacht.

A sooty pays a visit

We are going to have to reduce our electrical usage from now on. Ben's just confirmed that the starboard solar panel has died in the night, probably corroded internally. We've still got one panel left, and of course the engine will pump extra amps in if necessary. Not to mention the borrowed tow generator which is tucked away under the cockpit. At least little *Snow Petrel* is a low budget yacht. No fancy radars or microwaves to suck the juice out of this baby.

I settle back down to page 991 of 'London'. It's a great read, even though I've never been to that city. Matt wants to start it after me and I've got only 308 pages left.

DAY TWENTY-FIVE: 12 FEBRUARY
2100 HRS

We sailed right through a small Low centre today with 35 knot head winds, but thankfully it's settled down for the evening sched. I've arranged to try talking to Barbara on *New Zealand Maid*'s 4417 mHz channel tonight.

Once Ben has finished talking to Mike he retunes for me and wriggles out of the radio cave. I call once and wait. Bingo, it's her voice bouncing down to us from the ionosphere straight into my cramped little space. This is the radio frequency that most Kiwi fishermen use, but they should all be in bed by now so I'm hoping it's a reasonably private conversation. It's the first time I've

The enigmatic moods of the Southern Ocean always kept us guessing

heard her voice since we escaped the pack, and she has plenty to talk about. But there's a lot of static tonight, with an approaching Front, and we miss a lot of each other's news. Mindful of our marginal battery power, I sign off as her words dissolve into the crackling airwaves.

Radio transmissions are a science of their own. Talk to any ham operator and he'll have you baffled in an instant. Propagation issues, wavelengths, SWR meters ... it's a jargon all of its own.

The marine bands work in wavelengths which each suit a specific distance and time of day. The high frequency HF sets use fairly strong power outputs, usually between 70 and 150 watts. Using a 4 mHz frequency can be good for say 500 to 800 miles at night when the signals can be bounced off the ionosphere. For longer range calls, the eight or even 12 mHz bands are better. Generally Mike and Ben used these.

On New Zealand Maid *our set was nearly vintage. Bullet-proof but still old. It pulled a mere 35 watts, and topped out at 4 mHz. On our way south Mike had helped Barbara out with the odd call by relaying her voice through a short-range VHF channel onto his big set. 'Patching her through' was his jargon. Those VHF calls were pretty public though, audible to anyone in southern Tasmania who happened to have a VHF on scan.*

So this direct call was a special one, rubbing home the fact that we were getting much nearer.

We face the building greybeards of the Furious Fifties

DAY TWENTY-SIX: 13 FEBRUARY
0530 HRS

Getting hit by a Front like this is better on the morning watch than at night. The wind has just suddenly backed from west to sou'west, and cranked up another notch. It's now 40 gusting 50 knots, and Sooty can't hold her. We're rounding up often in the quartering seas, even with triple reefed main and virtually no genoa. It's a wild ride, averaging over seven knots, which is our theoretical maximum hull speed, and I love it. When Ben comes on at six we'll probably dump the main completely, but meanwhile the seas aren't dangerously huge and we're eating up the miles. Whoopee!

DAY TWENTY-SEVEN: 14 FEBRUARY
0430 HRS

We've had 30 hours of gale force westerlies, and at last it has started to ease a little. But even though it's now down to 30 knots the sea state has been steadily building. The waves have become teenage greybeards, I guess, pushed up by consistent westerlies over distance and time. Every now and then we get hit by a slammer, and if things don't ease soon, we'll need to turn more eastwards to take them on our aft quarter.

I felt sorry for Ben when he came on watch last night. The portapot must have tipped over during a part-broach on my watch, and when he went to the head before coming on watch, there was a smelly mess leaked onto the floor. It's the first time that has happened, as it has always been lashed into place, so something must have worked loose.

The first I knew of it was the sight of his very white face in the companionway holding the whole smelly thing out at arms' length. Then it was another twenty minutes with a bucket. I did offer to clean up, but he figured he might as well finish it.

What is more disconcerting is the GPS. It's died in the night, probably the aerial. Simply keeps flashing a message at us – POOR COVERAGE. Luckily we've got a backup handheld which can be mounted in the dodger. And if all else fails we'll become like sailors of old again, grabbing sun sights with Ben's sextant. He's a wizard at celestial, much better than me.

We did our first ocean race on New Zealand Maid *in 1991. The boys were crew. It wasn't a huge race, only 450 miles from Napier on the New Zealand East Coast to the Chatham Islands out in the Roaring Forties. We were proud of our freshly acquired second-hand satnav receiver, which could hopefully pinpoint our position once every four hours or so. GPS was a newer and vastly superior invention then, well outside our price bracket.*

One of my strongest recollections during that race was 16-year-old Ben sitting with me in the cockpit identifying fifty navigational stars from memory. And to top it off, proceeding to do a three point star plot. Self taught.

1600 HRS

It's happy hour and we're taking bets again. *Snow Petrel* is still barrelling along in this strong westerly, and we reckon it must be a record 24 hour run. Over the last couple of hours the blue sky and sun have reappeared and all is well with our little world. We're so happy with our progress that we've even decided to drink the last three cans of beer today. Matt has justified it as a delayed celebration for re-entering the forties during the early morning hours.

At the moment we're logging 7.2 knots, and the GPS has been showing over six knots all day. The bets are on Mike's calculated run when we give him our position tonight, which will be faster than today's noon to noon run which included some of yesterday's slower stuff. I make my guess 154 miles, and Matt reckons even more – 156. Ben is calculating for a while as he sips his beer. I hate it when he takes more time than us. It usually means he'll win. When he comes up with a conservative 148 miles, I'm surprised. He has taken into account the fact that we were steering 15 degrees off course for some of the day, so our point to point will be less than the actual distance run. None of us are too concerned about the outcome though – the prize is only our last can of soft drink. And from where I sit, the smell of Matt's two loaves of bread baking in the oven seems heavenly.

With the sun out, the cockpit temperature is up to 13 degrees, and we'd have our jackets off if it wasn't for the odd wave slopping into the cockpit. Sitting out here talking is such a treat. Matt has nearly finished 'London' now too and we're all discussing it. We've read our way through most of that box full of books, so we start quizzing each other on the ones we haven't read.

2100 HRS

Ben has won the bet of course. Mike has given us a sched to sched run of 147 miles. But Matt and I don't mind. Matt even cooked us a pudding tonight to go with the soy mince lasagna. How he keeps on cooking up these great meals in such a lively galley, I don't know. Sure, I stand by to stop things from sliding around. Probably his greatest motivation is the automatic immunity from dishwashing obligations. And the guarantee of a decent meal too, I guess. He has experienced my feeble efforts.

Tonight I talk to Barbara again, direct from the *Maid*'s steam-driven radio. The signal is much better tonight, probably because we now have only 297 miles to go. She sounds really excited and we discuss possible arrival times. It would be nice to guarantee an arrival in two days but Mike is predicting head winds so we can only guess.

We are all beginning to get 'channel fever'.

During Ben's days as a navigating officer with P&O they used to talk about suffering 'the channels', or 'channel fever', on the final days of a voyage. No high temperatures or sweats, just a restless urge to complete the journey as the English Channel drew nearer. It's a great name for that feeling which grabs us all near the end of any voyage, so the term has stuck. Except in our case it was the D'Entrecasteaux Channel we were hanging out for.

DAY TWENTY-EIGHT: 15 FEBRUARY
1100 HRS

The wind has hauled around towards the nor'west but we're still eating up the miles. Sooty is beginning to play up now. Maybe he's got 'channel fever' too. Every now and then he suddenly alters course. It's rather irritating attention-seeking behaviour, so I clip on to the backstay and have a look at him. Poor old chap. He's been working so hard all this time but he's losing his grip. The swivelling mechanism which locks the wind vane angle has a set of cogs and dogs which aren't quite meshing correctly. I secure it with a lashing, but from now on we will have to re-lash it each time we adjust the course. Meanwhile Ben has had a positive reversal of fortune. For days he has been struggling to receive weather faxes because his cheap computer stubbornly refused to boot up. Now suddenly it has burst into life and delivered him a wonderful prognosis showing moderate winds for the next few days.

And to cap it off, he pops up for his noon watch with the news that our noon run is 148 miles. We shake out the last reef and unroll the genoa fully before I wander below to my book. Life is wonderful today.

2330 HRS

Summer has returned at last. I can sense a hint of the Australian desert heat in this northerly air. Even now, sitting in the cockpit with a full moon beaming down, the thermometer reads 14 degrees. And Matt logged it at 21 during his sunset watch.

Now that the breeze has dropped to only 10 knots I am trying to cajole every fraction of boat speed out of the sails. A tweak here and there, handsteering to over-ride Sooty's lazy light wind yawing. Tonight I feel like an America's Cup skipper, extracting the best possible performance as we climb towards the final layline.

DAY TWENTY-NINE: 16 FEBRUARY
1200 HRS

This morning at six, Ben succumbed to our lust for speed. The wind had become really fickle during my watch, so he fired up the engine. According to our estimates we still have about 30 hours of fuel, more than enough to push us through this area of calm into the breeze on the other side. Even now I can see a hint of nor'easterly cats'-paws ruffling the water. Our noon run was 117 miles and we have only 85 miles left before we enter the Channel.

Now that I'm off watch, I'm bringing my mattress on deck for an airing. And stripping off to get some sun. It's 22 degrees now. And we'll almost certainly be home tomorrow.

It's so nice to be padding around in bare feet and singlets. I boil up for a good wash and shave. Ben announces that he's going to shave off his beard,

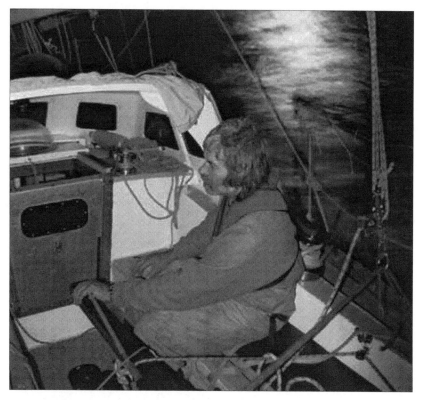

Hand-steering in the moonlight watch

but Matt and I try to persuade him not to. He looks rugged and handsome now that his awful crewcut has grown a little. We plan a happy hour of wine and nibblies this afternoon, and settle on a 1500 hr arrival time for the authorities to clear us in.

As if to emphasise how near we are to land, a visitor buzzes in. A blowfly, heading straight down the hatch. It must be blowfly heaven down there among the delightful smells of unwashed clothing.

DAY THIRTY: 17 FEBRUARY
0400 HRS

How often do we suffer headwinds as we get close to our destination? There must be something wrong with the law of probabilities. Tonight we are bashing our way into a mean head sea. Ben and Matt decided to dump both heads'ls during their watch change so now we're motorsailing with the main sheeted hard in. Spray is driving across the windward deck.

Ahead, slightly off the port bow I can see Cape Bruny light. How many mariners must have fixed their compasses on that landmark over the past eight score years, calling all hands to brace the yards for the haul up the East Coast maybe, or hardening up a little for the course to Cook Strait. Closing my eyes I can visualise the towering convict-built lighthouse, now merely a monument to bygone years, while its solar-powered usurper blinks away on the nearby clifftop.

I have joined the ranks of those ancient mariners this morning, as the first hint of pink lightens the eastern sky. Another landfall from strange and distant shores.

1130 HRS

When we talked last night, Barbara had decided not to bring *New Zealand Maid* to greet us. Unless she could organise a good crew, the *Maid* would be a handful to get in and out of her tight marina berth. Instead she's coming out on *Baudin*, with our marina live-aboard neighbours, Pete and Dell. We're ahead of schedule now, already half way up the channel and I can't raise her on the VHF. My cell phone batteries are flat so I've finally managed to call her via sat-phone, the most expensive short-range phone call I've ever made.

She's going to re-schedule Customs for 1330 hrs and is on her way now for a rendezvous. In the distance we can see not just one sail approaching but four. We guess for a while which boats are out to greet us. With binoculars we recognise *Kara, Aerandir* and *Tamahine,* all tucked in behind *Baudin* as a guard of honour. *Baudin* is first to take up position on our flank, Barbara on the foredeck looking wonderful, her red hair streaming in the breeze. She's close enough for conversation, and tells us that *Snow Petrel* looks great, looks as if we've just come in from a day sail. We call back excitedly, exchange key information and a little banter, before our little flotilla finds a natural formation for the final miles home.

1330 HRS

The business of clearing customs and quarantine always seems to act like a punctuation mark at the end of a voyage. It adds a finite point of closure, like a full-stop.

Conscious of the babble of voices and laughter above us on the dock, we hurry through the paper-work and gather the already bagged rubbish for the quarantine officer. Given that our only landfall has been largely organism free, we have nothing to declare except a few bottles of wine. Our official reception is one of cordiality and mutual respect.

The welcome sight of Barbara at the bow of *Baudin*, her red hair streaming in the breeze

The moment Matt has been waiting for as he pops the cork and delivers an exclamation mark!

Matt has been itching to open the champagne but Ben and I rein him in. We spring ashore to be greeted by handshakes and hugs. Barbara is right there, with a huge hug for us all, and I can't resist nibbling her tantalising neck

At home aboard *New Zealand Maid* again, as the party begins

in the process. If the boys feel a tinge of regret at recently failed relationships and the lack of a welcoming partner, then it doesn't show on their faces. Surrounded by a hubbub of noise, Matt insists we return to *Snow Petrel* for the final ritual.

It must be the best shaken champagne bottle ever to be uncorked. Its contents spray us all, even those watching from the dock, leaving only a few drops for our mugs. As closures go, Matt has delivered an exclamation mark!

EPILOGUE

And Later ...

This book nearly wasn't written. It owes its existence to the Global Financial Crisis. Not that I had any shares, but a couple of jobs fell over so I had time to think. And write.

It had been fermenting in the recesses of my mind for nearly three years, masked by Matt's movie. After all, whoever heard of a book being written after the movie. It's always the other way round.

The thinking put a perspective on the trip and its outcomes. It was a lot more than a six week family summer cruise. The experience opened some new doors for us all.

21 FEBRUARY 2006
FOR JOSH

We've been back for only four days when we hear the story. *Hugo Boss* was surfing at over thirty knots and the greybeards were building ahead of a shocking weather system when the mast fell over. In his bunk, Josh heard the bang only a split second before a spreader stabbed through the deck just a metre from his head. A million dollar carbon fibre spar to be cut away in a big hurry. Either that or leave it to bash a hole in the hull.

So there they were, wallowing in big seas still 1900 miles from Cape Horn. And at 53 South – that's about as far from civilisation as you can get. The only option was to rig a jury mast, and re-cut some sails. So they did, and by the time we got the message they were surfing again at 22 knots, covering

Josh sets sail for Cape Horn aboard the flying Open 60 *Hugo Boss*

300 miles a day with nothing but a stood-up boom and a couple of cut-down sails. How come Josh has all the fun?

It certainly made *Snow Petrel*'s six knots and 149 mile personal best seem a bit ordinary. And we had a whole mast up.

17 JUNE 2006

FOR MATT

All four off us are on the stage, and the clapping has barely stopped. Clapping mostly for Matt. A full house. And all standing. It's been the world premiere of his debut movie, 'Snow Petrel Down Under', and the opening night of the Longest Night Film Festival in Hobart's State Theatre. Already there are several extra screenings planned.

We are up for question time, and Barbara is fielding a question on how she felt as we sailed away. It's the first time she has expressed in front of me that she was gutted. She's always put on such a brave face about the whole trip.

Matt has found his niche at last. We knew he would one day. This movie was edited on a laptop in *New Zealand Maid*'s fo'c'sle, night after night during the past four months. It has been such a learning curve, but what an achievement. No wonder Screen Tasmania selected it from among the international selection as their star choice. And so, unwittingly, he has made us stars too.

5 FEBRUARY 2007
FOR US ALL, A SOBERING PERSPECTIVE

It is 54 South, not even half way to Cape Denison. Aboard the 70 foot aluminium schooner this is a nightmare turned real. Outside, it is hard to tell where water ends and air begins. The boat has become unsteerable. Inside, the noise is deafening and the motion violent. The entire hull is vibrating, an all-enveloping sensation which has already begun to loosen the rigging-screws on the mainmast shrouds.

For Ben's friend, Dave Pryce, the owner-skipper, this is the worst storm he has ever known, and he's sailed around the world three times. The wind is a constant hundred knots, and though he doesn't know it yet, somewhere above the clouds overhead a satellite is registering wave heights of 21 metres. For his eight charter passengers, who between them have paid enough to buy three *Snow Petrel*s for the excitement of sailing to Cape Denison, this is no longer exciting. It has crossed that fine line between exciting and terrifying, as they lie strapped in their bunks.

Abruptly the decision is made for Dave. The vibration has undone the propeller shaft coupling and the vessel is now effectively engineless. This year's crop of Cape Denison penguins will not be seeing any yacht anchored in their little boat harbour.

16 OCTOBER 2007
FOR BARBARA

There is a 25 knot following wind, a quartering sea and a two knot south-setting current, and *New Zealand Maid* is loving it. Alone in the cockpit, Barbara is back in the groove too. A slither of moon hangs in the western sky and there are whales about – she can hear them exhaling even though they aren't visible. Humpbacks, almost certainly – they are migrating southwards from Queensland on the same track as us. Except that we will be halting at Tasmania, while they will be continuing on *Snow Petrel*'s old track.

The *Snow Petrel* trip has been a catalyst for Barbara and me to modify our big heavily rigged gaff ketch for two-handed sailing. We no longer can expect the boys to crew for us and besides, we're happy just with each other's company. So this winter voyage to warm northern waters has been made easier by the addition of self-tailing cockpit winches, an electric anchor winch and electronic autopilot. And a roller furling heads'l of course. We see the investment as one towards our future. Sailing into our old age.

28 DECEMBER 2007
FOR BEN

The world's southern-most town of Ushuaia lies nestled in a steep-sided channel not far from Cape Horn. This morning, without any due ceremony, a 60 foot aluminium sloop has cast off its lines and is easing into the fairway. Ahead, only two or three days away, lies the Antarctic peninsula. Aboard, one of the four eager-faced charter guests turns his head toward the 33-year-old skipper. 'Where do I stow these lines, Ben?' he asks.

Another door has opened for Ben, one which channels a lifetime of experience and learning into an opportunity to share his passion. And, above all, a recognition of his qualities as a person who can deliver.

1 JANUARY 2008
FOR ME

My tent makes an awful din in this gale. It moans and flogs. My drink bottle has iced up too. Shades of déjà vu.

There are eight of us down here, camped on the snow outside the tiny field hut at Cape Denison. I'm the only one who has been here before, which is possibly why I'm deputy field leader. We're an eclectic mix of photographers, an archaeologist, a conservator, a doctor, an electrician and heritage carpenters. All selected by the Mawson's Huts Foundation to work on the program of stabilising the heritage structures.

The weather has been astoundingly kind to us during the fortnight since our arrival by helicopter from *L'Astrolabe*'s flight deck. This is only our second severe blizzard. We have another 17 days to complete our principal goal of extending the Sorensen's field hut to include a bunk room and field lab. There is still a lot to do, including a mass of guy wires to strap it down into solid rock. But I'm sure we'll do it.

22 AUGUST 2008
FOR THE FUTURE ...

It has been a long and difficult labour, but as one of New Zealand's top young women sailors, Sara Roberts has learned to cope with physical hardship. Through tired eyes she sees a pink plump body and pair of testicles lifted into a world of light. At her side, Josh Tucker is ecstatic. Already, the two have decided on a name: Nathan.

Our first grandchild looks likely to be destined for a childhood of sailing adventures. Already his bedroom is overflowing with boating toys, pirate books and even a boat-themed patchwork quilt. His parents, four uncles and both sets of grandparents all have boats which will be shaping his early sea experiences. Even his great-grandad is still building boats ...

17 JANUARY 1967
... FROM THE PAST

I'm sitting on the end of the bowsprit, one leg hooked around the bobstay and an arm around the forestay, immersed up to my chest in seawater with each plunge into this head sea. My job is to furl the jib. It's something I can do with my eyes closed.

New Zealand's Cook Strait has a mean reputation. It has been Dad's idea to do this double crossing with my brother Warren and me, from Picton to Kapiti Island and then back to D'Urville Island. An overnighter. As a fourteen-year-old, I don't think of it as a bonding exercise – just an adventure.

Our 25 foot vintage straight-stemmed cutter has no safety rails so Dad has run a rope from cockpit to shrouds, and looped a bowline around our chests for makeshift harnesses. We have no liferaft, just a tiny plywood dinghy. And no radio – the VHF hasn't been invented yet. This nor'wester is gusting 30 knots and rising.

*

What goes around, comes around.

APPENDIX ONE:
SNOW PETREL ACCOMMODATION PLAN

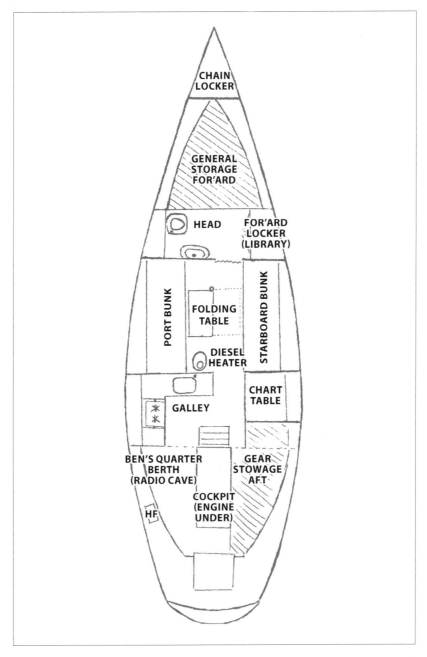

NOTE: Any diehard sailor-readers lusting after further juicy details about *Snow Petrel* should navigate their way onto Ben's blog site 'Snowpetrel Sailing'.

APPENDIX TWO:
BEN'S 'TO DO' LIST
Compiled two weeks before initial proposed departure date

Jobs to be completed before departure by Jon (J), Ben (B) and Matt (M)

INSIDE AFT
Weld in rudder bracket (B)
Shaft lock (J)
Cover for shaft so aft area under cockpit can be used for storage (J)
Install HF radio (B)
Strap down battery (M)
Install autopilot (B)
Lashing points for gas bottle (M)
Screw in hardwood battens for lashing to in quarter berths (and fwd) (M)
Leecloth (M)

GALLEY AND CHART TABLE
Install saltwater pump (J)
Change over FW pumps (J)
Galley light (J)
Strap up radio (M)
Lockdown for chart table lockers outside and under (M)
Fire blanket (B)
Secure stairs (J)
Main hatch securing bolt (M)

MAIN SALOON
Lock down floorboards (J)
Table lashing (B)
Lash in battery box (B)
Leecloths (M)
Speakers? (M)
Cabin heater top (B)
Chisel in official number (J)

TOILET AND FOR'ARD
Lashing points for toilet (M)
Check floor lockdowns (M)
Screw battens to fwd locker (M)
New securing bolts for fwd hatch (B)

ON DECK
Self steering -new vanes – extra supports – weld on weight (B)
Aft hatch lockdowns (B)
Tiller to shim and bolt (J)
Winches and clutches to install under dodger and holes to drill (B)
Strengthen dodger with ring frame?
Staysail sheet leads (B)
Waterproof dorade boxes (M)
Tighten lifelines and install dodgers (B)
Seal all windows (M)
Put name on stern (B)

RIG
Swap over masthead halyards (B)
Modify furler details (B)
Spinnaker block? (B)
Topping lift block? (B)
Spectra lashing for caps and backstay (B)
Inner forestay lashing? (B)
Lash in radar reflectors (B)
Runner lashings (B)
Trysail block (B)
Reefing system (B)
Weld up gooseneck (B)
Drill holes in spinnaker pole (B)
Deck struts (B)
Boom brake
New bottlescrews for caps and backstay (B)

GLOSSARY

Aft   The back area of a vessel.

Barometer   An instrument which reads air pressure.

Beam   The side of a vessel. (Also a term used for its width measure-
                         ment.)

Beating   Sailing as close into the wind as possible, and tacking.

Bow   The front of a vessel.

Bowsprit   A short spar extending horizontally in front of a yacht.

Bergy bit   A large piece of ice which has broken away from a parent iceberg.

Bulkhead   A structural 'wall' inside a vessel.

Chart   A navigational map.

Chine   A sharp angle in the cross section of a hull.

Cockpit   A deck-well area where most crew work takes place.

Companionway   The ladder and hatch entranceway to a yacht's cabin.

Coms   Abbreviated slang for radio communications.

Crampons   Strap-on spikes for boots, supplying grip when walking on ice.

Danbuoy   A floating upright pole and flag, used to locate a person in the
                         water.

DDU   The shortened name for Dumont D'Urville Base.

Dead-reckoning   Navigating on assumed speed and direction, not sun-sights.

Displacement   The total weight of a vessel (equal to the water it displaces).

Dodger   A shelter built above cabin level for cockpit protection.

EPIRB   Emergency position-indicating radio beacon. Radio beacon,
                         detectable by satellite for rescue purposes.

ETA   Estimated time of arrival.

Fetch   The distance between a vessel and the windward shore.

Fo'cs'le   The forward cabin (derived from the 'forecastle' of ancient ships).

Forestay   The wire-rope supporting a yacht's mast to the front of the hull.

Furl   To take a sail down and make it secure.

Front   A turbulent area between converging air masses of differing
                         densities.

Genoa   A large sail, set in front of the mast.

GPS   Global positioning system. An instrument using low orbit satellites
                         for navigation.

Growler   A nearly submerged large piece of decayed ice, dangerous and
                         difficult to see.

Gunwale   The deck edge.

Helm   The steering position.

IAATO   International Association of Antarctic Tourism Operators.

Inflatable   A collapsible small boat, with an internal pump-up bladder.

Jib	An outer head-sail.
Katabatic	Heavy cold air flowing down a slope.
Knot	One nautical mile per hour, or just under two kilometres per hour.
Lee side	The downwind side of a boat or landmass.
Moruroa	A Pacific island where French nuclear testing took place until 1996.
Optimists	A class of small sailing dinghy designed for children.
Parallel	A line of latitude in whole degrees. Each is a ring, parallel to the equator.
Pitching	A motion in which the bow rises high before burying itself deeply.
Planing	A condition in which a vessel skims across the surface of the sea.
Port	The left side of a vessel.
Quarters	Either side of the stern.
Ratlines	Ropes or wooden rungs rigged as ladders up the shrouds. (Pr. Ratlins)
Reaching	Sailing with the wind from one side.
Reefing	Reducing sail area to compensate for a rising wind.
Rhumb line	The most direct route on a standard chart between two points.
Running	Sailing with the wind from directly behind.
Sched	Scheduled report. A pre-arranged time and frequency for radio communications. (Also Sked)
Scope	The ratio of anchor chain length to depth of water.
Seaway	The rise and fall of waves and swells.
Sheet	A rope used to control the angle of a sail.
Shroud	A yacht's wire side stays, supporting its mast.
Soundings	Depth of water, measured from a very low tide (datum level).
Spreaders	Spacer bars which hold wire side stays away from the mast.
Starboard	The right side of a vessel.
Staunchions	Vertical thin posts around the deck-edge, supporting life-lines.
Stern	The back of a vessel.
Stem	The structural rise at the bow, where two sides are joined.
Swell	A rise and fall of the sea resulting from waves no longer pushed by wind.
Tabular bergs	Very large icebergs with wide flat tops.
Tacking	Sailing a zigzag course into the wind, switching from side to side.
Tiller	A shaped lever connected to the rudder, used for hand-steering.
Tinker	A brand of inflatable dinghy designed for ease of boarding from the water.
UTC	Coordinated universal time. The time zone set at Longitude 0, British time. (Also Geenwich Mean Time or GMT.)
VHF	Very high frequency. A compact radio for short range conversation.
VMG	Velocity made good. Adjusted speed to a point, allowing for off-course angles.
Windward side	The side of a vessel or landmass which is exposed to the wind.

ALSO BY JON TUCKER

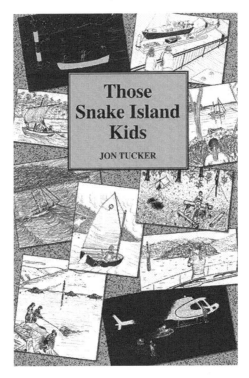

When Jake persuades his family to embark on a camping sailing holiday on a small Tasmanian island, he is mostly interested in pirate fantasies and his small home-built sailing dinghy. But he doesn't plan on events which are to leave him isolated with his brother, sister and two Kiwi friends Ultimately, after being forced to dig deep into their personal reserves, the treasures that they all gain are very different from the ones that Jake had set out to find.

This multi-layered and highly satisfying book is being hailed as a contemporary classic of the Ransome genre, and has become internationally popular with young and old readers alike.

PRAISE FOR *THOSE SNAKE ISLAND KIDS*

'*This first book in a promising new series reflects the sensitivity to environmental issues that you would expect from a writer who recently sailed with his sons to the windiest place on earth.*'

Ann Packer, The Listener (NZ)

'*Jon Tucker has written the book which I had always wanted to write but never did. He has done a spanking good job of it too!*'

David Bamford, The Arthur Ransome Society

'*It is incredibly important to realise that sometimes kids just want to immerse themselves in a good old-fashioned adventure story. Jon Tucker delivers one with his second book ... inspired by true events and places as well as his own life in which he and his wife raised five sons aboard their ketch...*

An engrossing romp of a read which you don't have to be young to enjoy.'

Dani Colvin, Sunday Tasmanian

For further information, visit www.nzmaid.com

ALSO BY JON TUCKER

Finalist for the Australian Environmental Award for Children's Literature, 2015

Young Fin has always been passionate about fishing, so when he discovers an illegal net full of undersized fish in Sydney's northern waterways, his first reaction is to empty it. The subsequent events turn a joint Kiwi-Australian boating holiday into a rather more complex experience.

'In a complex and well-written tale of friendship and sailing, Jon Tucker gives a big nod to the tales of Arthur Ransome, while creating a modern-day adventure as thrilling as those books of older times. A clever and rewarding read.

Elizabeth Jolley. Editor, North Pole News, USA

ALSO BY JON TUCKER

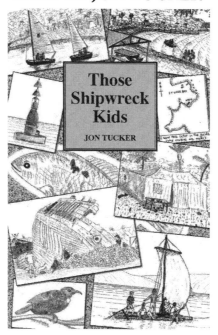

When a Tasmanian sailing family anchors near a wrecked hulk in New Zealand's Marlborough Sounds, the kids discover a strangely abandoned campsite nearby, with plates of uneaten food and children's toys still visible under the mould and cockroaches. Their curiosity leads to an investigation which adds a layer of intrigue to their anticipated fun-filled experiences in an unfamiliar foreign land.

A thought-provoking Ransome-inspired tale with strong appeal to adventure-loving readers in the nine to ninety-nine age bracket Underlying its clear environmental message is the conclusion that freedom and responsibility go hand in hand.

As a parent or teacher it is a very rewarding read, with much food for thought when it comes to nurturing both our environment and our children, advocating the importance of a child's adventuring and fiercely independent spirit. These books have a place in both the environmentally focused classroom and the more confident upper primary reader's adventure collection.
Lisa Hoad, Children's Book Council of Australia

ALSO BY JON TUCKER

When three Tasmanian children meet a couple of home-alone kids who live on an old barge in New Zealand's Bay of Islands, they soon find themselves caught up in a conflict with one of the local oyster-farmers over the spread of plastics in the local inlet. The outcome is a triumph of lateral thinking and a signal to youngsters everywhere that it is possible tobring about changes that will help shape the future of the world.

A fast-paced boating adventure that brings the Ransome genre squarely into the 21st century, and promises to capture the attention of even the most reluctant reader.

If your children are interested in sailing, wildlife or the environment (or even if you'd like them to be interested in any of those things!) get them this book! And read it yourself.
Dr Duncan Hall - UK author/reviewer

The fourth in a fantastic series of sailing adventure books for children ... brilliant books that children will love, with plenty of boating tips subtly included.
Viki Moore, Yachting New Zealand Director

Made in the USA
Columbia, SC
07 April 2019